Netflix's Speculative Fictions

Netflix's Speculative Fictions

Financializing Platform Television

Colin Jon Mark Crawford

LEXINGTON BOOKS
Lanham • Boulder • New York • London

Published by Lexington Books
An imprint of The Rowman & Littlefield Publishing Group, Inc.
4501 Forbes Boulevard, Suite 200, Lanham, Maryland 20706
www.rowman.com

6 Tinworth Street, London SE11 5AL, United Kingdom

British Library Cataloguing in Publication Information Available

Library of Congress Cataloging-in-Publication Data Available

Library of Congress Control Number: 2020949866

ISBN 978-1-7936-2528-1 (cloth)
ISBN 978-1-7936-2530-4 (pbk)
ISBN 978-1-7936-2529-8 (electronic)

Contents

Acknowledgments

This book is dedicated to the innumerable friends, family members, colleagues, and most importantly mentors who have guided, encouraged, and challenged me over the years. I would like to specifically thank first and foremost Dr. Marc Steinberg for his unwavering dedication to helping me develop and push this project in new and unexpected directions. I would also like to thank Raphaele Hubert, Maral Sotoudehnia, Lex Konnelly, Keiko Hart, Elena Pnevmonidou, and CindyAnn and Reuben Rose-Redwood for your endless generosity and support over the years. None of this would have been possible without each of you.

Introduction

NETFLIX'S SPECULATIVE FICTIONS: FINANCIALIZING PLATFORM TV

What is a show worth to Netflix? Really, what is the value of any given title in Netflix's catalogue? How does Netflix's debt-intensive, vertically integrated model for platform TV work? Does it actually work? These were the questions from which this book has emerged as a journey into the intersecting worlds of technology, culture, and finance industries. I quickly realized that any possible answers to such questions must simultaneously consider a dizzying constellation of factors. On the one hand, there are technically measurable factors such as licensing and/or production, labor, marketing, content delivery infrastructure maintenance, localized subscriber pricing, debt financing structures, and viewership data. But on the other less measurable hand, qualitative industrial factors such as title-specific brand power and longevity, "free-promotion" from fan discourses and content, industry literature and criticism, various international market pressures, and so on are much more difficult to account for or ascribe value to. The truth is, the "value" of any given title to Netflix is incalculable because of platform television's complex matrix of affective, financial, technological, and sociocultural characteristics. The company rather views its titles as enterprising investments—risks—of varying sizes and its content library as a portfolio, all of which serve the project of the Netflix brand; the Netflix *story*. Users and investors alike thus subscribe, not only with their capital but with their faith in the value of Netflix as a service and a stock.

Realizing my initial research questions were unanswerable has, however, been deeply generative, forcing me to find new lines of approach and to synthesize emergent methodologies in efforts to better understand the new

1

media economics of Netflix and the expanding platform television industry. The result is this monograph. What I hope to show is that the feasibility of Netflix's economics is also incalculable because they take place in the future worlds of finance. In the eyes of Netflix's executives and investors, such futures and worlds are malleable and of course potentially wildly profitable if they are able to bring into being the visions they project. With this perspective, this monograph examines Netflix's discursive and rhetorical mutations over the decades, as it has grown into a global force in culture, technology, and finance industries, ever in service of such specific futures.

In trying to grasp the staggering scale of Netflix's operations—192.5 million subscriptions worldwide, market valuation of $216 billion, hundreds of millions of hours of video streamed daily, annual content budgets of up to $15 billion, and $27.8 billion in long-term debt and liabilities as of July 2020—I turned to the company's financial communications for answers. In Netflix's financial documents, however, all I found were more stories; stories of innovation, convenience, and efficiency; stories of strategic debt and cash burning in service of continued expansion and future returns. This is Netflix's most compelling, interesting, and expensive original program; a *speculative fiction* for speculative audiences of investing actors–venture capitalists, investors, banks, creators, and users.

This book offers a close reading of the financial (hi)story of Netflix, exposing the central importance of narrativity, performative language, rhetoric, and affect which drive the speculative worlds of global finance, technology, and well, *television*. Where Netflix once represented a unique startup-style amalgam of these industries (finance, technology, and film/television), its model for platform television has inspired widespread competition from the largest technology, telecom, and media conglomerates the world over—Apple, Amazon, Google, Facebook, Disney, HBO, NBCUniversal, the Criterion Channel, Tencent Video, Baidu's iQiyi, and Alibaba's Youku, to name but a few. Billions in investment, with no guarantee of return, is now the norm for delivering TV and film over the internet at such scale. Returns on investment in the landscape of platform TV are anything but clear. This consideration is most interesting, and perhaps concerning, for the tech giants. Indeed Amazon burns over $700 million per year to provide its TV platform Prime Video, just to ingratiate users into the Amazon e-commerce ecosystem; as the company's CEO Jeff Bezos has famously stated, "when we win a Golden Globe it helps us sell more shoes" (Levy 2017; McAlone 2016). What work then does platform television do for say Apple, Google, Facebook, or Tencent? In the age of the platform, television is playing increasingly important roles as a financial technology in various economies and ecologies of attention (Citton 2017). Ubiquitous computing and connectivity have evidently produced *ubiquitous televisuality*, with its attendant economic systems of value generation: subscriptions, advertising, and brand association as the Bezos quote above clearly demonstrates. What this monograph adds to the study of Netflix is that the company has streamlined the financializability of television by cutting out advertising and vertically integrating over the internet. Netflix has done this through language; through selling a story and a future.

What I want to show is how Netflix's financial communications have played a vital role in inspiring the vast shifts toward platform television seen today. Netflix's narrativization of value elucidates the desires, fantasies, and organizations of its investing actors seeking to bring into being the value they describe and project. By asking what television delivered to "any internet connected device at any time" means in the context of our accelerating techno-financial capitalism of the twenty-first century, this book offers unique insights into how we got here, and where we might be going. Particular to this analysis of Netflix is an emphasis on performative financial language and discourse. The coming chapters excavate the company's now well-worn "startup to tech giant" narrative at a deeper and more granular level to examine the rhetorical and affective charge of its communications, and the billions of dollars of capital, and billions of hours of content such discourses continue to mobilize.

Over the past two decades, the culture industries of film and television have, like everything else, mutated importantly under the dominant forces of technology and finance industries. Our capacity to deliver moving-images over the internet at scale has evolved from minutes of video of varying quality—pornography, YouTube—into (endless) hours of high-quality content/ IP delivered consistently to myriad devices and applications, bringing forth new worlds of economic possibility. I define this relatively new, online video landscape throughout the book as "platform television" and use this term (as opposed to Streaming or Subscription Video On Demand) to keep in mind the platform logics of exchange and extraction, and the ubiquity of televisuality produced by hyperconnectivity. The expansion of platform television production and consumption brought forth by the online distribution revolution is simply unprecedented (Curtin, Holt, and Sanson 2013). For example, Netflix alone produced 371 new titles in 2019 compared to the 292 new series produced by the entire U.S. television industry in 2005 (Elliot 2019; Netflix 2020). The longer history of this industrial expansion is worth examining, as the potential speeds and scales at which film and TV could be distributed, consumed, produced, and financ(ializ)ed have each expanded rapidly with the help of the internet. In the eyes of Netflix and its investors, its market is, in essence, *the waking hours of the world*, as CEO Reed Hastings has stated "we actually compete with sleep, and we're winning" (Raphael 2017). These are the speculative fictions of Netflix and the financialization of platform TV.

It is worth noting here that this monograph is concerned with Netflix's deeply American culture and operations. In spite of the majority of the company's revenue—$3.25B of $6.09B in Q2 2020—and subscribers—120 of 193 million—coming from outside "UCAN,"[1] Netflix remains overwhelmingly U.S.-centric, ever focused upon the American power centers of Wall Street, Silicon Valley, and Hollywood. To put it another way, the company depends upon growing its international user base and funneling such flows of "global" revenue and data back into the United States to translate these value inputs into financial and informational capital which can be in turn reinvested into Netflix's global operations. It is of course no coincidence that the dominant language of global finance is not only the U.S. Dollar but also American English. This book, therefore, focuses its critique upon such U.S.-centered narratives of value and grammars of financial power.

The central drive of this monograph is to expose and analyze the *financializing work that language performs* in the convergence of film, television, finance, and technology industries. More specifically, it outlines and interrogates such language as narrative discourses of value organized and sustained by the emergent technological and financial logics of neoliberalism and platform capitalism throughout the twenty-first century. To do so, this book examines the corporate rhetoric and financial communication—*Investor Lore*—of one of the world's largest proponents of platform TV, Netflix, to elucidate the central importance of language and narrativity in the unprecedented new organizations and movements of content and capital seen today.

This excavation of Netflix's performative communications considers the new ways in which the media forms of film and television are framed, mobilized, and valued in the age of the digital platform. For the purposes of this book, I adapt Timothy Havens's concept of industry lore: "The conventional knowledge among industry insiders about what kinds of media culture are and are not possible, and what audiences that culture will and will not attract" to put forward the concept of *investor lore*, which I define as: the *emergent discourses* among *investing actors* about what kinds of *user experiences* are and are not *valuable,* and *which users those experiences* will and will not *engage.* Emergent discourses, investing actors, user experiences, value, engagement. These are the new keywords necessary to broaden the study of media, culture, and finance industries in the age of the digital platform. *Investor lore* expands the reach of the concept of industry lore to examine a broader range of actors, discourses, and narratives emerging in contemporary media industries and economies. Alongside *investor lore*, this book also outlines and integrates theories of corporate communications, media convergence, financialization, and platform capitalism. Such integration provides a hybrid framework through which we can begin to unpack how Netflix's narrative discourses of value have come to mobilize vast quantities of content and capital.

As the media industries of technology, culture, and finance fold into one another, so too do their metaphors. The work of disambiguating, interpreting, and excavating such layered metaphors and discourses is now a necessary and generative methodology for the study of these media industries which increasingly permeate everyday life. At times they align, at times they obscure. For example "IP" stands for Intellectual Property but also Internet Protocol. "Stream" connotes a flow of revenue as well as the delivery of content, compressed into data packets delivered to user devices. "Performance" can refer to that of an actor on screen(s), but also of a stock that financial quarter (also on screens). "Interest" is the attention or appetite of the user-audience, and is also the profit-generating component of debt financing. "Programming" is both the curation and flow of digital content libraries and the code behind various screens. "Projection" is both market forecasting and the play of light upon the screen—or more commonly now, the glow of our screens illuminating us. Are we *con*tent or con*tent*?

"Speculative Fiction" is thus no longer just a genre, but a potent metaphor for financialized modes of production exacerbated by platform capitalism, where value is increasingly mobilized and generated through investments of *faith* in increasingly speculative narratives and temporalities of capital investment, exchange, and return. While such processes are not particularly new, they are now operating at unprecedented speeds, scales, and wagers which we must understand and resist. The concept of speculative fiction in the title of this monograph follows the Marxian concept of fictitious capital, in which the value is derived and reproduced more so from increased circulations of capital as opposed to material production. These new forms and flows of capital—financialization—are ever present today and indicate the outward spiraling and expansion of late capitalism; a neoliberal fantasy of profit without production (Jameson 1997, 246, 249). The drive of capitalism to reproduce itself has been exacerbated by digital ubiquity, as our increased capabilities for new speeds and scales of data gathering and exchange perpetually accelerate the production of new markets upon which to speculate.

Despite the glut of information generated by our new computational powers, the most profound, profitable, and inexhaustible new market generated in this process is that of uncertainty itself. Like language, uncertainty is perhaps one of the only other "universal" human conditions. Mitigated ever inadequately by our impulse to narrativize, to understand, preempt, and prepare, humanity is interminably found, or perhaps lost, wanting. The unknowability of the future drives life in both anticipation and dread, and it gives meaning to stories, and now increasingly gives value to markets. In the current era of expanding financialization, layers of risk and uncertainty have been folded into the speculative fictions of global finance; commodified into value-producing wagers through layers of derivative contracts. Our ability to invert risk and uncertainty into value and profit is due in large part to advances in computing and communication technologies and the construction of networked global information infrastructures. Such powers constantly accelerate the speeds and scales of exchange in hopes to consequently increase the speed and scale of value generation and accumulation.

The marriage of technology and finance industries signals the mutual reinforcement of a technocratic, financialized, economic logic that is increasingly speculative and fictitious. These clouded abstractions of the digital and the financial carry deep material, social, and cultural consequences. Digital cultures and experiences are produced, experienced, felt, and embodied by people; they mobilize, monitor, and monetize various resources, services, products, ideas, ideologies, aesthetics, and most importantly *experiences*. Our networked concepts of power and information have been literalized by the digital in all their opportunity and injustice.

In the tech industry—itself always already financialized—buzzwords such as scale, optimization, connectivity, disruption, personalization, user experience, and artificial intelligence each rest upon the tension drawn between measuring and valuing the experientiality of the present and the potentiality (uncertainty) of the future. Silicon Valley's desire for prediction, automation, and scale signals the utter objectification and commodification of such uncertainty; of *experience* itself, reducing and instrumentalizing the complexity, immeasurability, and beauty of everyday life into data at the service of capital. This is platform capitalism, both landlord and intermediary, always observing and quantifying in hopes of bringing into being predictable and thus profitable patterns of reality.

This fixation upon "experience" driving intertwining culture and tech industries today is a twin question of narrative and language. In consumer society, the most important element of any project pitch or brand is storytelling. Everything must be a story—moreover a story and *experience* of value. While this logic is nothing new, the speed, scale, and stakes of this game have dramatically outpaced the rest of the economy through the ever faster, ever more powerful instruments of finance (and) technology. This inflationary techno-economic process of financialization has been performatively reified and accelerated through performative language and narrative discourse: investor lore. There is of course a reason Marx's term fictitious capital likens these financializing processes to fiction and narrative; they are relational, imaginative, compelling, and potentially valuable. The same uncertainty that gives value and meaning to our stories, and indeed life itself, has been instrumentalized, datafied, and financialized in platform capitalism.

Trafficking exclusively in a market of stories, which of the major tech firms better represents these new narrative discourses and logics of value than Netflix? With a user base of over 192 million paying members, hundreds of millions of hours of content streamed every day, and revenues, debts, and obligatory payments climbing into the tens of billions, Netflix evidences the emergent scales, speeds, and stakes of value derived from today's complex entanglements of tech, finance, and culture industries. Such new forms and flows of value are ever-shifting assemblages of capital, language, data, culture, debt, information, content, infrastructure, labor, and sociality.

For this book, I take aim at the communications of Netflix executives and investors as the loci of discursive and financial power fueling the machine of Netflix. The company's investor lore is a piece of speculative fiction masquerading as a documentary; a new story of value constructed for and projected to an investing audience of shareholders, potential investors, users, financial, tech, and entertainment industry analysts and journalists. Netflix's narrative discourses of value have organized new assemblages, movements, and questions of media value through the convergence of technology and culture industries. Reading and questioning such narrative discourses is imperative to understanding the emergent organizations and movements of capital, culture, content, and control today.

With this political-economic philosophy in mind, this book examines the speculative fiction of Netflix's story so far. From its early days as a DVD-rental-by-mail startup to today, Netflix has sought to capitalize upon industrial convergence and media circulation through the already existing structures of finance: venture capital, debt financing, and stock value. The company's twenty-two-year history has produced an abundance of texts evidencing this constant project(ion) of a meta-narrative of value, building up to and after its initial public offering in 2002. This story has proved successful insofar as the company has managed to maintain its growth. By becoming a dominant global vehicle for the distribution of digital video entertainment, the company has also become a dominant site of financial exchange and accumulation for investors, at least so far. On the other hand, the perceived success and value of their streaming-platform "studio" model has sparked a massive wave of competition, putting the sustainability of the company and its narrative to the test of increasing competition. In the intensifying drama of the streaming market, audiences of users, creators, and financiers are witnessing the rising action and ensuing complications of an increasingly uncertain future. Amid rising pressure, the question now must be asked is, "Will Netflix *the company* continue to be renewed season after season?"

I hope the methodology and critique found here can help media industry scholars and thinkers untangle how Netflix, and perhaps other streaming platforms, have performatively mobilized capital through communicating narratives of potential value over time through narrativizing financial discourses. Central to Netflix's communications has been the company's brand of superior user convenience and experience of home—and now mobile—film and television entertainment. User *convenience* pertains to its nonlinear, subscription-based, ad-free distribution models, while user *experience* deals with the discourses of personalized, enjoyable, and meaningful practices of "engaging" and "participating": browsing, viewing, rating, discussing, and debating. These discourses are constantly reinforced by narratives and images of the user or "member" seamlessly enjoying—frictionlessly consuming—a library of increasingly "original" Netflix content on "any internet connected device."[2] This motif of Netflix as the provider of the most convenient and enjoyable experience of television and film consumption crucially reframes practices of viewing as designed user experiences: products of technology. Such narratives have found broad validation from Wall Street, with the Netflix stock performing extremely well over the past decade, dominating the hybrid market of platform television the company so proudly claims to have invented.

The new relationships between the investing audiences of users, financiers, and talent (labor) constitute this emergent investor lore and its new narrative discourses of value. Each of these actors is invested in how technology is reshaping film and television production, distribution, consumption, financing, and valuation. While the focus of this book is platform TV, this user-investor-labor nexus is a central pillar of platform capitalism and its discursive production of value more broadly. By this I mean that investors and workers are now not only financiers and producers but also users in varying capacities within these increasingly convergent industries. In turn, users are also investors, financiers, audience members, producers, and workers (Terranova 2004). Each of whom invests time, attention, data, energy, information, infrastructure, capital, and sociality into the mechanisms of the platform, all-the-while generating returns of ever more data, content, and thus capital—or so the story goes. Each of these "investments" and "returns" is crucial component of the mercurial web of (media) value today, entering into and moving through the now ubiquitous architectures of digital platforms.

Despite the prominence of Netflix on Wall Street, little critical attention has been paid to Netflix's financial and investor-facing communications. In analyzing the projection and leveraging of Netflix's brand as a leader in both technological innovation and now popular cultural production, I examine how television and film content is increasingly reframed, reimagined, and revalued as financializing technologies in platform capitalism. Despite the vast changes brought forth by the convergent industry of platform television, Netflix's promise of superior user experiences of home and mobile entertainment has remained the bedrock of its brand from the outset. I view this as a call to examine how such narratives of user convenience and experience have mobilized billions of dollars of capital from the world's investing class and finance industry. In what follows, I take Netflix's own words as my primary objects of analysis. The company's financial documents, press release archive, investor relations materials, and executive interviews, alongside trade literature from tech, finance, and culture industries are brought together by this book to examine the meta-narrative of value Netflix has crafted for itself, and projected to the world of finance. Formally, I quote many passages at length from such sources to display and analyze Netflix's rhetorical strategies of persuasion, and the work they perform in making new forms and flows of media value in platform capitalism.

Since 1997, Netflix has been telling the tale that their ability to provide, predict, and guide user experiences will further translate into their ability to provide, predict, and guide future capital in the forms of profit margins, stock value, and returns on investment through theoretically ever-increasing inputs of subscriber revenue and data. These are the new narratives, temporalities, and mediations of value that come with the digitization and subsequent datafication of the everyday leisure practice of watching; a new financialization of spectatorship itself. Under the name of convenience and user experience, Netflix has been able to extract, expand, and mobilize complex new constellations of increasingly flexible structures of use, exchange, and labor value. Data, attention, time, information, intimacy, infrastructure, capital, content, labor, and sociality are increasingly measurable and thus increasingly valuable, as they are monitored, circulated, monetized, and exchanged through the ever surveillant mechanisms of platform capitalism. This datafication of seemingly every practice of everyday life indicates new organizations of power; mobilized, justified, and sustained by emerging discourses of value. Where an application or platform provides a "valuable" service or convenience to its user, the deeper motivation is the data and thus potential *value* that the user represents: paying attention and investing their digital behaviors into the platform. This extractive logic exhibits a fundamentally neoliberal, financializing ethos which translates behavior and attention into data, under the belief that it can translate such data into capital. The user has thus emerged as the idealized, surveillable,—if not self-surveilling—subject of a technoliberalism run amok.

Dominant tech companies and their various platforms (Facebook, Amazon, Apple, Google, Microsoft, Netflix, Huawei, Tencent, etc.) are the architects of this insidious and inherently financializing economic model. The case of Netflix is particularly profound and unique, however, in its entangling of surveillance, technology, entertainment, and capital *through its provision of narrative;* the speculative, expressive, communal, informational mode of humanity itself. It is the intrinsically human reliance upon sharing and consuming stories which Netflix now extracts, commodifies, and financializes through its platform model. What this book hopes to achieve is an excavation of the underlying, meta-narrative of media value which has brought these conditions into being.

Before each of these major tech giants rose to their current scale, they sold *narratives* of future value to financial audiences of venture capitalists, angel investors, industry insiders, and banks. Those plotting words mobilized the initial capital necessary to launch and eventually sustain corporate operations; shifting, adapting, and mutating the narrative to organize, justify, and project certain futures. This is the performative cultural logic of our increasingly platformed economy. It is thus imperative to analyze the discourses of platforms and their foundational narrative myths to understand, unpack, and ultimately resist these increasingly surveillant, financializing, and concentrating new organizations of value and power. This book, therefore, focuses on Netflix, and more specifically the narrative discourses of value it projects within its financial communications and investor relations materials. In looking at this company's communique with the finance industry specifically, I hope to elucidate and excavate the layers and structures of belief which mobilize and sustain unprecedented flows of capital into the platform economy, and platform television industry in particular.

I interrogate the language and rhetoric which constitutes the layered meta-narrative of value which has driven Netflix's growth. In so doing, I examine the multiplicities, mobilizations, and monetizations of meaning and metaphor which have expanded and entangled traditional economic concepts of exchange, use, and labor value into the nebulous cloud of *user value: data, capital, content, credit, debt, attention, time, information, infrastructure, labor, and sociality.* Working with the rich metaphor of the stream, the platform is perhaps more akin to a hydroelectric dam, managing, manipulating, channeling, and harvesting momentous new flows and inputs, in hopes to transform, generate, and sustain energy and *value* in perpetuity.

To begin to unpack these new narratives of media value, I first lay out my conceptual framework which combines theories of media convergence, platform capitalism, human-computer interaction (HCI), and financialization. I present and explain these concepts as mutually constitutive industrial, technological, and political-economic forces which have produced the conditions of platform capitalism seen today. Expanding and orienting the idea of industry lore toward financial discourses—investor lore—is a necessary turn if we are to understand media value in the age of the platform today. "Investment" no longer pertains only to finance capital, but also data, attention, information, time, sociality, participation, and "experience." In platform capitalism—and thus platform television—users, financiers, executives, journalists, academics, creators, and programmers are all *investing actors* shaping new forms and flows of value, capital, data, and content. The idea of media value is thus a complex and multiplicitous matrix of financial, technological, sociocultural, and affective characteristics, produced by and for the aforementioned investing actors and stakeholders. To rethink media value we must ask who *invests* what, when, where, how, and why? What is exchanged, risked, or sacrificed in such interactions? What are the ideologies that justify such flows of capital, content, and code?

The coming chapters employ a textual analysis of sorts to examine the discursive, rhetorical, and narrative nature of Netflix's investor lore, identifying the narrators, story arcs, figures, themes, and motifs crafted throughout Netflix's history. While much has been said of Netflix's "disruptive" practices, virtually none have critically considered the company's *discourses* surrounding and justifying such practices as inherently valuable. With this in mind, I examine Netflix's communications as influential and performative utterances of value creation and financialization. This book thus looks at the industrial discourses of streaming as the production and legitimization of specific knowledges which justify and sustain the new forms and flows of capital, content, and data. As Chris Weedon writes "Discourse[s] are ways of constituting knowledge, together with the social practices, forms of subjectivity and power relations which inhere in such knowledges and relations between them" (1987, p. 108). In this era of platform capitalism, industry lore must also include the study of the interrelated and essential roles of financialization and convergence as discourses central to media industry operations, both today and into the future.

When thinking of performative speech, a declaration, promise, or contract is inherent in the performative utterance: to say *and do* what you say, either simultaneously or in the future (Austin 1962). As Butler has elaborated, social realities and meanings are brought into being and legitimated through the repetition of promissory, performative acts including and beyond speech. This reifying relationship between speech, text, and action is at the heart of the concept of discourse as a networked body of knowledge, produced and reproduced through its performance. This book thus demonstrates how such an understanding of (financial) discourse can be productively applied to industrial practices also. This theoretical understanding of performativity lends itself to media industry studies, as industrial convergence is brought into being not only through industrial practices but also importantly through such discourses which *prefigure and legitimate such practices as valuable.* The power and scale of the company and its operations are directly related to its ability to convincingly communicate and project potentialities of value. This is critical as such discourses, if successful, will mobilize initial investments for expansion, and future investment to feed the insatiable appetite for scaled growth at the very heart of capitalism in the age of the platform.

Given the high proportion of corporate and financial source materials this book examines, it is worth noting my debt to Ken Hyland's "Exploring Corporate Rhetoric: Metadiscourse in the CEO's Letter" (1998) in which he aptly notes:

The CEO's letter is widely seen as a promotional genre, designed to construct and convey a corporate image to stockholders, brokers, regulatory agencies, financial media, and the investing public [. . .] Generally written as a signed personal letter, the document has enormous rhetorical importance in building credibility and imparting confidence, convincing investors that the company is pursuing sound and effective strategies. So, while research suggests that investment decisions are mainly based on financial data [. . .], the CEO's letter is widely read [. . .] and its contents are an important means of validating quantitative measures. [. . .] Thus the letter is a highly rhetorical product that can have a major impact on a firm's competitive position. (Hyland 1998, 224)

Under my umbrella category of *corporate communications*, I engage a range of primarily investor-facing texts and media such as the Netflix press release archive and company blog, financial reports, CEO letters, executive interviews and statements, popular and trade publications, webcasts, and keynote speeches. This book also performs an archival function, as Netflix has erased all its press releases prior to 2015 from its media archive; demonstrating the instability, ephemerality, and thus the importance of documenting such discourses. Throughout the book I quote and juxtapose many of these corporate texts at length in order to display, analyze, and excavate the new discourses of value and industry lore they put forth. In examining Netflix's *investor lore* in this way, I hope to expose the discourses and narratives of value held by a range of stakeholders: executives, investors, shareholders, venture capitalists, users, and creative and tech talent (platform capitalism's favorite word for labor). As critical discourse analysis necessitates, I examine each text's site and date of publication, author(s), key terms, ideological stance, style, and intended audiences in search of answers to these emergent questions of media value. Discourses constitute society and culture, and must be analyzed and interpreted as inherently performative and political (Fairclough and Wodak 1997; Van Dijk 2001). Through this methodology I showcase how this range of media sources and texts work to create performative discourses: networks of associations and knowledges reinforcing the convergent and ever-evolving identity of Netflix and the value of its products and services (Lury 2004).

Netflix's corporate strategies and communications must be understood and analyzed as highly influential discourses from its position as a dominant platform in the streaming-video-on-demand (SVOD) industry, as "successful firms become models for capitalists, stimulating corporate trends, business literatures, state policies, and transnational regulatory environments" which "guide our ability to imagine the size, spread, and generality of capitalism" (Tsing 2009, 154). In an entertainment market where tech and media giants are racing to replicate many aspects of Netflix's platform model, this is all the more relevant. Netflix is the current industry leader by all measurements, and embodies and expands the spread of platform capitalism through its performative language; through its speculative fictions.

The shift from audiences asking "What's on TV?" to "What's on Netflix?" signals vast structural changes in the distribution, organization, and consumption of film and television, now distributed and consumed as *digital content*. In Amanda Lotz's recent book *Portals: A Treatise on Internet-Distributed Television* (2018), she maps the developments of platform TV as three major and interconnected affordances: (1) Nonlinear programming, (2) subscription revenue models, and (3) vertical integration. Contrary to the legacy television model of advertising revenue based upon viewer demographics, portals can rely on subscribers to provide revenue, precisely *because* of the data they collect regarding taste and user behavior. As competition heats up within the SVOD industry, dozens of platforms are clearly racing to (1) provide nonlinear programming, (2) extract subscriber revenue and data, and (3) vertically integrate, as producing, promoting, and distributing proprietary or exclusive content is now becoming a necessary practice to remain competitive and profitable in today's media landscape. Platforms are thus becoming conglomerates, and conglomerates are becoming, or acquiring, platforms in efforts to survive under the data-driven logic of the day. Building upon Lotz's overview of the structure of platform TV, I examine *how* this structure has been formed, communicated, narrativized, and projected as *valuable* over the past two decades.

Vertical integration, often notable and quantifiable evidence of industrial convergence, is nothing new, although it has developed in interesting ways under platform capitalism. Indeed the modus operandi of the "startup" is to mobilize venture capital and often staggering debt to develop IP, scale growth, and raise perceived value to a point in which such IP, *and debt,* are acquired by quite simply, a larger fish. We can see this convergence and integration through mergers and acquisitions (M&A) in the SVOD industry, with Disney's acquisition of streaming company BamTech and controlling shares of 21st Century Fox/Hulu, with AT&T acquiring TimeWarner, and with Netflix purchasing the IP universe of Millarworld as but a few weighty examples. Even Netflix itself is a product of these increasingly common processes, as the cofounders Reed Hastings and Marc Randolph—brought together by acquisition in 1996—carpooled to work in Silicon Valley in 1997, brainstorming ideas for future companies as both of their positions were soon to be made redundant by yet another upcoming merger which would pay out both men handsomely.

These moves indicate the rising prioritization of concentrating capital and consolidating control of IP, be it software technology or cultural content, the gap between the two ever-shrinking. Here these ideologies and practices of the tech industry are clearly converging and subsuming those of Hollywood, as media and entertainment conglomerates are increasingly operating like startups and tech companies. This M&A logic of vertical integration in (and of) tech and entertainment industries is indicative of the tendencies toward media convergence and monopolization in platform capitalism. Furthermore, this raises important concerns not only for market controls such as pricing power over consumers and security questions regarding the collection, control, and use of increasingly intricate user data, but also broader, murkier questions regarding the provision of culture; namely film and television. Yes, there has been an expansion and diversification of niche "narrowcasted" content for user-audiences, but this perhaps misdirects attention and concern from the fact that these structures of content provision (any combination of production, promotion, licensing, or distribution) are becoming increasingly surveillant, extractive, and concentrated in the hands of a shrinking few.

Reframing Netflix's communications as actively narrativizing texts brings to the surface the power of rhetoric and the centrality of language in increasingly convergent culture, technology, and finance industries. Placing these industries and their convergent discourses in conversation with one another is fundamental to understanding and critiquing the logics and narratives of value which justify, organize, and govern platform capitalism.

CONCEPTUAL FRAMEWORK

The conceptual framework through which I analyze the investor lore of Netflix exemplifies that the convergence of technology and culture industries are discursively performed under the financializing logics and narratives of potential value creation in platform capitalism. Thus the provision—financing, licensing, production, promotion, and distribution—of platform television is creating and controlling unprecedented, novel forms and flows of value. Data, behavior, attention, time, content, information, infrastructure, and sociality are now translated and financialized from inputs into investments similar to those of capital, credit, debt, and labor. Each of these new forms and flows of value is organized and justified through narrative language; a clouded assemblage of rhetoric, code, images, and voices. *Each text performs a story.* Importantly, this discursive performance is both aimed at and reproduced by an *audience* of investing *actors*: users, executives, investors, shareholders, venture capitalists, and talent. Labeling this broad group of stakeholders as investing audiences and actors and their communications as *investor lore*, is helpful in excavating and unpacking the narrative discourses of these datafied and financialized forms and flows of value. For the purposes of this book, I focus primarily upon the formal financial discourse of Netflix's executives aimed at current and potential shareholders to examine the company's unprecedented mobilizations of capital through investment and debt financing. However, while I focus upon financial and executive communications here, I believe the framework of investor lore is also applicable and useful for studying other groups of investing actors, such as users, fans, creative and tech labor, journalists, and researchers. Through shared reliance upon digital technologies and infrastructures, each of these groups' *emergent discourses, user experiences, engagements,* and notions of *value* interact with these giant industrial actors. Whether you like it or not; whether you subscribe or pirate; you have a relationship with Netflix. The same goes for Google, Amazon, Facebook, Apple, and so forth by virtue of their scale and ubiquity (one might even say inescapability). The very language we use to understand our relationships with these giants is a part of investor lore at work.

Acknowledging the depth and broadness of the concepts and theories of performative language (*and finance*), industrial convergence, platform capitalism, and HCI, the remainder of this introduction seeks to highlight the emerging connections between these concepts as interrelated and interdependent instruments of today's increasingly surveillant and financializing capitalism. I believe these concepts, theories, and discourses must also converge, intersect, and overlap if we are to begin to make sense of the myriad complicities and complexities of Netflix and the new narrative language of value in platform capitalism.

The Performative Language of Financialization

The interrelated processes of convergence, financialization, and cultural production are sustained by metaphor, rhetoric, and discourse. Here Arjun Appadurai's *Banking on Words: The Failure of Language in the Age of Derivative Finance* (2016) lends particular insight. The argument of this book is that the 2007/2008 financial crisis was "primarily a failure of language," a violation of the ethical, legal, and linguistic contracts which constitute the infrastructures of finance (2016, 1). Appadurai puts forth the idea that the logic of the derivative—and financial exchange more broadly—hinges upon the performativity of language. He argues, "The link between derivatives and language turns on the question of promises, which I view, following Austin, as one of the class of performatives, linguistic utterances that, if produced in the right conditions, create the conditions of their own truth" (2016, 6). Drawing parallels between the abstracting nature of both language and capital, Appadurai examines their intersection, and the material consequences they bring about through their performative mobilization. Thus he calls for a *textual analysis of the derivative*; and a deconstruction of the discursive interplay between language and capital. Heeding such a call, this book examines Netflix's performative financial language with a similar attention to promises: the potential accrual of future value in exchange for immediate investments. I examine Netflix's multisited investor lore as a performative discourse, which "must be understood not as a singular or deliberate 'act,' but, rather, as the reiterative and citational practice by which discourse produces the effects that it names" (Butler 1993, 2). By constantly reiterating and citing specific discourses and promises of value, Netflix seeks precisely to bring into being the forms of value that it names. Netflix's investor lore remains a networked project of rhetorical performance, aimed to instill faith from users, investors, and labor in the myriad forms of *value* the company projects to each of these actors and audiences.

I am interested, however, in the tension between the success and failure of such performative speech acts and discourses, as such utterances *become* performative when they succeed but constative when they fail. The retroactive nature of such discourse analysis must examine its content as more porous and nonlinear than perhaps previously thought. Indeed the new media "logic" (discourse) of the long-tail hints yet again at the new and intersecting temporalities of success and failure in converging finance, culture, and technology industries. The speculative (narrative of) value of cultural products and company stocks in platform capitalism are thus suspended in the cloud—an unsteady state of potentiality, performativity, and constativity. In the face of such uncertainty, the language which justifies such cultural production is again, always a promissory one of financial, market value; an aspirational orientation ever toward a successful performative. It is thus no coincidence today that both linguistics and finance borrow from the arts the metaphor of *performance* as such enactment of potential, necessarily displayed for an audience. Who better represents these reflective foils of performance than Netflix?

In finance, the term *Story Stock* is used to describe the inflated value of stocks that have achieved such desirability through communicating their scalability and potentiality to investors. In other words, story stocks belong to the firms who have crafted the most effective *investor lore*. Investopedia elaborates: "Story stocks often garner substantial media coverage. Because of the abundant attention, a story stock may attract heavy trading volume for many months, until a new contender displaces it. A few story stocks may achieve great success, but most *fail to achieve their promise*" (2019). This quote further elucidates the performative and promissory discursive logic of finance, particularly in relation to story stocks of which Netflix is a rare success, thus far. Moreover, the so-called FAANG group of stocks—the acronym given to Facebook, Amazon, Apple, Netflix, Google by influential finance commentator Jim Cramer—in particular have become synonymous with successful story stocks. These technology firms have been successful because of their ability to craft and sustain a narrative, a speculative fiction, of value for the investing class.

Returning to Appadurai, he repeatedly engages Max Weber's *The Protestant Ethic and the Spirit of Capitalism*, expanding the idea of "the market" as a social system based upon faith or religious subservience through which society seeks to mitigate the brutal uncertainty and unknowability of the future. Media and technology scholars such as Ed Finn and Ian Bogost similarly argue that the new faith system of our times is one of digitality, technology, and algorithms, coined as a "computational theocracy" in Bogost's essay *The Cathedral of Computation* (2015). As stated previously, this computational rationale is quite literally indebted to—and also constitutive of—a financializing rationality. One need look no further than to the relative silence on the floor of the New York Stock Exchange for evidence of the dovetailing of technology and finance; with the noise and drama which long defined Wall Street automated away; the figure of the bustling white-collar broker seemingly disappeared by the algorithms and network infrastructures of the cloud.

Appadurai's phrase "the hybridization of ideologies of calculative action" furthermore describes how new technological forms of "calculability" are mobilized and monetized within finance industries. These new capacities and instruments of measurement provide new forms of data and information, which in turn allow for new forms, categories, and markets that can be traded, exchanged, and gambled upon, both now and in the future. Finance scholar Michel Callon similarly notes how these technologies and models are in many ways performative in the very act of their modeling, bringing into being the phenomena they seek through finding ways to measure them. This performative conceptualization of finance argues that the capacity to performatively "calculate" is an industrial practice directly connected to power and the discursive framing of knowledge, numbers, models, statistics, and markets. The discursive power given to data and statistics is present in all facets of economics but has taken on a new level of influence with the rise of finance capitalism, setting the stage for the dominance of data in platform capitalism. As technologies make data increasingly collectible and calculable, the positive feedback loops and dialectics of technology and finance become ever more apparent; apparently ever more valuable.

As mentioned earlier, technology firms have long been directly reliant upon the financial structures of venture capital, investment funding, debt financing, public offerings, and so on. These tools and structures of finance thus determine whether many technologies or innovations have the capital to grow, come to market, turn a profit, and, therefore, survive (Appadurai 2016). While the portmanteau FinTech is defined by Investopedia as the improvement of financial services through technology and automation, these industrial forces increasingly subsume more and more aspects of contemporary society and everyday life, which are datafied and thus in turn financialized. Perhaps we may ask, what *isn't* financial technology today? With this in mind, the following chapters show how these emergent logics and practices of tech and finance industries are framed in relation to culture industries, through the discourses of Netflix. Following Appadurai, I examine the *language* this media giant has used to perform, justify, communicate, and at times obfuscate such practices as *value-generating.* In doing so, I hope to elucidate the financializing power this language yields in the spheres of technology and culture industries within platform capitalism.

Industrial Convergence

Industrial convergence theory emerged in the late 1970s from the Massachusetts Institute of Technology's (MIT) Media Lab, led by Nicholas Negroponte (Fidler 1997, 25). Negroponte anticipated that communications, content, and computing industries would increasingly converge through shared reliances upon digitization, becoming ever more interrelated, intersecting, and overlapping as rates of technological development accelerated in the latter two decades of the twentieth century (Fidler 1997). The smartphone evinces this theory in many ways, as this single device now functions as not only a mobile phone, but also a computer, television, radio, newspaper, magazine, book, camera, credit card, MP3 player, game console, calculator, flashlight, notepad, and so forth. Such convergent consumer technologies are now the dominant intermediaries between people, media, and culture, and audiences and citizens are increasingly redefined and repositioned as users. The user is the primary figure of the twenty-first century; an idealized, atomized, self-surveilling, neoliberal subject. As industries continue to converge, the figure of the user is *essential* to the discourses and developments of the digital economy, and more specifically to platform television.

In *Convergence Culture,* Jenkins writes:

> By convergence, I mean the flow of content across multiple media platforms, the cooperation between multiple media industries, and the migratory behaviour of media audiences who will go almost anywhere in search of the kinds of entertainment experiences they want. Convergence is a word that manages to describe technological, industrial, cultural, and social changes depending on who's speaking and what they think they are talking about. (2006, 3)

Jenkins highlights the centrality of the digital platform within contemporary processes of industrial convergence as they accelerate new *flows* of content as well as new (*user*) audience behaviors. From popular services for social media, entertainment, ride-sharding, and advertising, to industrial manufacturing transportation, and supply chain networks, a range of platforms are now part and parcel of our increasingly digital economy (Srnicek 2017, 11). Such processes of convergence have been often described by the dominant catchphrase of Silicon Valley: "disruptive innovation" or more simply "disruption." Like convergence, the definition of disruption is in its essence the idea that technological innovations in digital computing can upset the strategies and practices of traditional markets and industries to find, save, and create new forms of value, increasingly in the form of data regarding the behaviors of users (Zuboff 2019). Convergence plus financialization equals disruption, the guiding light of platform capitalism.

Platform Capitalism: A Financial Technology

Platform Capitalism is the increasingly common economic model wherein data continue to become ever more valuable as resources, and platforms have emerged as the best and perhaps only suitable model for the collection, processing, and intermediation of such data as an industrial necessity and competitive advantage (Srnicek 2016). Srnicek notes how both the dot com crash of the late 1990s/early 2000s, and the recession of 2007/2008 were important moments of economic instability where financial capital—ever seeking its own reproduction—flooded into the tech sector, creating the conditions for the rise of platform capitalism, a marked evolution in postindustrial economics.[3]

This leads us to a deeper discussion of financialization, which Gerald Epstein defines as "the increasing role of financial motives, financial markets, financial actors and financial institutions in the operation of the domestic and international economies" (2003, 3; as quoted in Davis and Kim, 2015, 205). The explosion of the finance sector over the last thirty years is itself inherently linked to developments in computing and information technologies which allow for new rates and scales of financial data collection, organization, processing, and mobilization (Currie and Lagoarde-Segot 2016, 211). Netflix, like all tech companies, could not exist without these contemporary structures and instruments of finance capitalism: venture capital, debt financing, share distribution, and stock investment.[4] In the contemporary North American context, the *platform is always already financialized;* making the portmanteau FinTech always already redundant.[5] The simultaneous expansion of finance and technology industries has been co-constitutive and mutually reinforcing from the outset, as the parameters of technology define the rate and scale of financial circulation and exchange.[6] What the emerging literature examining platform capitalism fails to highlight is how financialization, technological production, and industrial convergence are functions of one another.

As technology companies have come to dominate the stock market,[7] the financial imperatives of convergence have been made apparent in the recent M&A of major computing and media companies (AT&T acquiring TimeWarner; Disney acquiring 21st Century Fox and thus a controlling percentage of Hulu). These M&As unsurprisingly evidence an industrial trend toward vertical integration and monopolization, in which the rise of the digital platform has exacerbated financial logics and promises of efficiency, scale, growth, and control (Srnicek 2016). These trends indicate how giant media and entertainment companies feel they must adapt (converge) into technology and telecommunications conglomerates to survive in a global digital economy where data is increasingly valuable.

Under platform capitalism, however, temporalities of value have importantly been re-oriented and skewed toward scaled growth and market share domination over immediate profit. The logic of the startup is indeed to "blitzscale" growth as fast as possible at whatever cost to sell its IP, data, and debt in a merger or acquisition, or recoup said debt over time by going public and further monetizing such services and products (The Economist 2019; Srnicek 2017). Indeed Uber, which was privately held until recently, has burned over $11 billion in its nine-year history hedging its bets (and debts) on precisely this model (Hawkins 2018). While Uber may finally prove to be a failed business one day, for those who invested early, the company was a very useful and profitable investment, as they were able to sell their stock options and walk away.

Disruption and convergence are part and parcel of the financial processes of investment, projection, speculation, derivative trading, merging, and acquiring. Such processes are importantly framed as *compelling narratives; investor lore.* The new temporalities of value production in platform capitalism thus fictionalize and financialize the future, postponing and hedging risk and consequence through gambling upon the performance of certain companies, ideas, and technologies in the markets of tomorrow. This tantalizing tale of fictitious capital has become the totalizing speculative fiction in which we live.

As massive tech platforms encroach upon seemingly all industries, it is important to examine how industrial convergence interfaces with cultural production. In platform capitalism, how does datafication and digitality affect the production and circulation of culture? Can major film and TV studios and distributors sustainably scale at the rate of tech companies?[8] Netflix certainly has proclaimed it can, and financial, technological, and cultural industries and markets have certainly listened eagerly. *The perceived reward is greater than the perceived risk.* The industrial practices—and communication—of Netflix's platform model for television and film have emerged as an increasingly popular narrative of value, of which my analysis takes aim.

Jameson's *Culture and Finance Capital* (1997) considers the ideological and theoretical teleology of financialization, arguing that it signals the logical extension or outward spiraling of late capitalism, a tellingly postindustrial and postmodern fantasy of "profit without production" (246).

> Any comprehensive new theory of finance capitalism will need to reach out into the expanded realm of cultural production to map its effects; indeed, mass cultural production and consumption itself—at one with globalization and the new information technology—are as profoundly economic as the other productive areas of late capitalism and as fully a part of the latter's generalized commodity system. (Jameson 1997, 252)

The inverse of the above statement is also true today I would argue, as any comprehensive *study of popular cultural production will need to reach out into the expanded realm of finance capitalism to map its effects*. This abstraction of profit generation through the instruments of finance is heightened for Jameson through the development of faster and more powerful computing technologies. As cultural production and consumption shift and converge ever-increasingly toward the digital and the financial, Jameson's prescient theorization is increasingly relevant in considering how technology and culture industries have converged through financialization.

In an analysis of another streaming giant, Patrick Vonderau's 2017 article "The Spotify Effect: Digital Distribution and Financial Growth" provides a contemporary examination of the convergence of media industries, finance, and platform capitalism. The parallels between Netflix and Spotify are manyfold. Both are online platforms lauded as "disruptors" of traditional media distribution, praised for curbing piracy, shifting media consumption to subscription-based streaming models, and engineering effective and taste-making recommendation algorithms. Vonderau's thesis is that Spotify uses convergent industrial practices from advertising, technology, music, and finance sectors to fold multiple markets into each other and generate value from potential loss. He employs Leslie Meier here, who notes "In a digital economy that favours 'free' or advertising-subsidized content, the big tech oligopoly is able to use cultural content as a loss leader and promotional medium in efforts to drive sales elsewhere" (Meier 2017, 162; as quoted in Vonderau 2017, 3). With this he examines how Spotify applies user data profiling and machine learning algorithms to mark and sell ad-space, for itself and others. While operating only on subscriptions, without "free," ad-dependent models, Netflix internalizes a similar strategy to gather data in order to personalize content suggestions for that user, an ever-increasing proportion of which are Netflix Originals. In short, this too is an internal advertising strategy. Both practices capitalize, mobilize, and monetize user taste and behavioral data through their streaming-platform models. Netflix's recommendations are ultimately pleasantly renamed and rearranged homepage advertisements at the end of the day. In the same article, Vonderau notes, "this present situation—where music has become data, and data in turn has become contextual material for user targeting at scale—invites reflection about the way songs, movies, or books are currently made accessible" (2017, 3).

The metaphor of the stream puts forth the image of content or services as data flowing seamlessly down from the cloud to your devices for your convenience and enjoyment (Holt 2017). However, we must interrogate this metaphor, for the stream flows both ways. As you use and consume platform services and products, a flow of your ever more valuable behavioral data is concurrently streamed back up to the cloud of that platform. Here, user experience, behavior, and participation are directly financialized, yes in the form of subscription and ad revenue, but perhaps more importantly in terms of brand equity, identity, taste, and loyalty, each of which is key factor in investment discourses and thus markets. This in turn makes user growth crucial, in terms of increasing existing user engagement and simultaneously adding new users; a constant hunger for more and more data to feed platform capitalism's insatiable appetite for *scale*.

> "Growth" here relates to the attempt to accumulate fictitious capital, in the sense of capital only indirectly related to the growth of real production. It is a strategy that does not primarily aim to turn songs (or audiences) into commodities but to treat them as a form of collateral that can be mobilized to secure loans. This is an investment in something yet to come, built on a "bit of fake-it-till-we-make-it hopefulness" where the hope is that, "at some tipping point, a different kind of advertising, one not based on immediate response but on investing in shifts of mood, opinion, and desire, of creating the grand illusions and stories that propel consumer life—and big media margins" will emerge. (Wolff 2015, 87, as quoted in Vonderau 2017, 13)

Here Wolff briefly touches on the new narratives and temporalities of media value which form and flow through culture, technology, and finance today. Indeed Netflix's business of storytelling *literalizes* Marx's concept of fictitious capital, a new financialization (of) narrative. Sociologist Randy Martin examines the debt instruments of finance as contractual—*linguistic*—obligations for *future* compensation, which mobilize *immediate* capital. In many ways, Netflix is using its *provision of culture as a debt instrument*, to mobilize capital, by turning both visual content *and* the practice of viewing into valuable data and projecting this data as a competitive edge to investors. As I will discuss further in my analysis chapters, this content strategy hinges, perhaps precariously, upon stability in debt and stock markets as sustainable financial instruments for capital investment, scaled production rates, and eventually profit. The similarities between Spotify and Netflix exemplify the convergence of culture, tech, and finance industries, as streaming platforms which create value through datafying the multidirectional flows of code, content, and capital.

User Experience: A Portrait of the User as Neoliberal Subject

In platform capitalism, the user has emerged as the idealized neoliberal subject, forced to offer their capital, data, information, attention, labor, and sociality to "participate," and "engage" in the "experiences" of contemporary life and digital cultures. It is through the figure of the user and the proliferation of consumer technologies that human behavior has become increasingly surveillable, measurable, extractable, and exchangeable (Zuboff 2019, 21). Insights from the fields of computer science and digital product design help frame Netflix's user-centric investor lore. Baumer and Brubaker's (2017) work on HCI and User Experience (UX) theory is particularly relevant here. They write:

> The third wave of HCI begins to grapple with life outside of professional and organizational work contexts. Moving beyond the workplace and productivity, computing takes on numerous varied roles: leisure, socializing, gaming and sport, sensing and expressing emotion, cultural production and meaning making, etc. As computing moved "off the desktop" into smartphones, mp3 players, cars, tablets, etc., it moved into myriad other facets of our lives. These developments constitute HCI in yet another way:
>
> 1. A human is a person engaging in (a set of) socio-cultural practices embedded within numerous broader contexts, including cultural, historical, political, organizational, etc.
> 2. A computer is a technological system that may consist of a single device, a constellation of devices, an infrastructure, or a more complex assemblage that arises from and is embedded within a particular set of contexts.
> 3. An interaction is the experience of leveraging a technological system in the course of an individually, socially, or culturally meaningful practice.
>
> (Baumer and Brubaker 2017, 62)

This understanding of HCI is deeply relevant and applicable to the stories of Netflix, streaming, and platform capitalism more generally, as the definitions of these terms are increasingly and necessarily reproduced by the discourses of the expanding technology industry. As technology "disrupts" and encroaches upon more and more aspects of everyday life, such "practices, systems, and experiences" of being are increasingly influenced by a philosophy of design centered around the figure of the user. The user is not abstract, but rather highly conceptualized, constructed, and idealized by programmers and designers as a specific type of consumer with a certain value within a potential market. In the case of Netflix the user is not only a paying subscriber, but importantly a member of a televisual and filmic taste community, informed by their data surrounding viewing practices, behaviors and histories, such as what you watch, where you watch, in what language, on what device, for how long, how many times, how you browse, and how you "engage" recommendations. Nir Eyal's widely circulated "hook model" for "habit forming digital product design"—external trigger, action, variable reward, investment, internal trigger, action, investment, and so forth—further illustrates how platform products, services, and experiences such as Netflix are created to encourage habit formation, in other words sustained flows of investment. Reminiscent of a narrative act structure—exposition, inciting incident, rising action, climax, denouement—the hook model seeks to bend user investments of interest and attention ever inward: an always false denouement inspiring habitual, circuitous user behaviors and associations. Where the descending numbers of the film leader's revolving beacon once anticipated a beginning, the autoplay countdown features on Netflix, YouTube, and other streaming platforms signal the endlessness of our new tech-driven ideology; a hook model for culture.

Where Netflix uses the different terms of "user," "member," and "subscriber" to describe its consumer base, I will use *user* from here on, to emphasize again the forms and flows of exchange and extraction inherent in the platform. Projecting a better *user experience* has remained the central feature of Netflix's discursive project to redefine practices of television viewing, consumption, and production. The following chapters show how subscriber growth has been the most directly correlated metric to investor faith, where the scales, rates, and projections of Netflix's user base growth has translated into stock value and thus the power to mobilize massive debt contracts and bonds for the company's operations. This book exemplifies how Netflix has built itself upon new discourses about the user as a consuming audience member. User subscription fees, behavioral data, time, attention, ratings, hype, critique, discussion, and sociocultural capital are now treated as inputs of value the company mobilizes and *reinvests in and for its operations and processes of financialization.*

Integrating these theories of convergence, financialization, and platform capitalism, and tracking their impact within culture industries, this book applies this conceptual framework to Netflix's investor lore. As platform capitalism produces new conceptualizations and potentialities of value: data, attention, time, information, infrastructure, engagement, labor, sociality and control, the theories outlined here provide a framework to excavate how Netflix has discursively crafted and employed this new narrative language of value; an increasingly speculative and fictitious capital.

OUTLINE

The structure of this book divides the history of the company into three "acts" which examine the dominant discursive and operational chapters of Netflix's story so far. Act I: What Is Past Is Prologue (1997–2007) examines Netflix's founding origin narratives, role in fostering the DVD ecosystem, initial public offering, and formative battle with rental giant Blockbuster (1997–2007). Act II: Hope Streams Eternal (2007–2011) covers Netflix's central role in the propagation of the SVOD ecosystem between 2007 and 2011, focusing upon how Netflix communicated the potential value of immediate, ad-free, subscription-based access to film and television content as computers became TVs and vice versa. Lastly, Act III: Networking the "Global" Original (2011–) interrogates the company's shift toward original programming and international expansion in the face of rising domestic competition. These acts are not separate or discrete, but rather build upon one another in a cascading narrative of value, projecting the potential of "innovating" and "disrupting" the media industries of rental video, television, and cinema. My analysis thus performs a close reading of Netflix's investor lore, identifying the emergent narrators, themes, motifs, and figures present in the investor lore of—as netflixinvestor.com boldly proclaims—"the world's leading internet entertainment service."

This chapter structure allows for a narrative analysis of the company's dramatic investor lore over the decades, excavating Netflix's corporate autobiography to expose the inner workings of its performative financial discourses. These acts are sutured together by the continuity of Netflix's brand identity as the provider of the best, most convenient home entertainment experience, but are notably distinguished by the operational and discursive foci of the company over time: DVD-rental-by-mail, streaming, and the two-pronged strategic shift to original production and global expansion.

Evident throughout Netflix's investor lore is the solutionist ideology of Silicon Valley which discursively frames or manufactures a "problem" which can be conveniently "solved" by a tech product or service, embodying the neoliberal logic of market creation as a means to mobilize value and capital, ever in hopes of profit. In this case study, I exemplify how Netflix was conceptualized as a "solution" to the myriad problems of Blockbuster and has also gone on to "solve" the inconveniences of television's linear scheduling, ads, and apparently now even borders. In doing so, I highlight and analyze the performative nature of such solutionist discourses as poignant examples of the new language of the growing streaming industry and platform capitalism more generally.

NOTES

1. Netflix's abbreviation for the region: United States and Canada.
2. Netflixinvestor.com, 2020.
3. See chapter 1 of Srnicek's *Platform Capitalism* (2016) for more.
4. From the outset Netflix's initial investments came from CEO and founder Reed Hastings himself as well as Silicon Valley venture capital firm WS Investments Inc (Crunchbase 2019).
5. For more on platform economies outside the North American context, see the work of Marc Steinberg, Jinying Li, Michael Keane, Julie Yujie Chen.
6. Not to mention the important role of public defense spending in the development of the U.S. tech industry.
7. Facebook, Apple, Amazon, Netflix, and Google comprise the "FAANG" acronym in finance discourse (originally coined by Jim Cramer of the Finance TV program Mad Money) as the dominant tech stocks on the NASDAQ exchange.
8. See *The Curse of the Mogul* (Knee, Greenwald, and Seave, 2011) for more on the contested financial logics of media conglomeration.

Act I

What Is Past Is Prologue (1997–2007)

In search of an origin story for Netflix, a narrative tool all successful and especially "disruptive" companies, founders, and CEOs must have at the ready, many different tales emerge. I include three accounts of Netflix's origins, as they function as expositional—albeit subjective and retroactive—"establishing shots" of sorts, introducing lead characters and narrators, the context of the scene, and inciting incidents which catalyze our protagonist's journey.

> The genesis of Netflix came in 1997 when I got this late fee, about $40, for Apollo 13. I remember the fee because I was embarrassed about it. That was back in the VHS days, and it got me thinking that there's a big market out there. So I started to investigate the idea of how to create a movie-rental business by mail. I didn't know about DVDs, and then a friend of mine told me they were coming. I ran out to Tower Records in Santa Cruz, Calif., and mailed CDs to myself, just a disc in an envelope. It was a long 24 hours until the mail arrived back at my house, and I ripped them open and they were all in great shape. That was the big excitement point.
>
> —Reed Hastings (Abkowitz 2009)

> While Reed was driving to the gym and pondering his [Apollo 13] predicament he realized the gym had the perfect business model for watching movies. Gym members pay a flat fee for unlimited use no matter how often they work out—why couldn't movie watchers just pay a flat fee regardless of how many movies they watched? And thus, Netflix was born. (Morgan 2016)

There's a popular story about Netflix that says the idea came to Reed after he'd rung up a $40 late fee on Apollo 13 at Blockbuster. He thought, What if there were no late fees? And BOOM! The idea for Netflix was born. That story is beautiful. It's useful. It is, as we say in marketing, emotionally true. But as you'll see in this book, it's not the whole story. Yes, there was an overdue copy of Apollo 13 involved, but the idea for Netflix had nothing to do with late fees—in fact, at the beginning, we even charged them. More importantly, the idea for Netflix didn't appear in a moment of divine inspiration—it didn't come to us in a flash, perfect and useful and obviously right.

—Marc Randolph, co-founder and former CEO of Netflix (2019)

Hastings positions himself in his origin stories as an average guy, a movie-lover, and a frustrated consumer fuming over a $40 late fee on his way to the gym. He also characterizes himself with a clever, entrepreneurial spirit which drove him to solve this issue, not only for himself but for as many as he can through new technologies or alternative business models. These quotes are distilled examples of the "disruptive" lore Hastings, and by extension Netflix, frequently put forth. Such brief scenes perform an efficient rhetorical function, offering a sense of narrativity and identity to the company, while positioning founders and CEOs as protagonists, and thus easily digestible, discursive interfaces for the brand (Lury 2004). Hastings's replacement of Randolph as CEO in 1998—with Randolph staying on as president until departing after the company's IPO in 2002—was also a strategic choice of not only leadership but *narration*. In Randolph's recent Netflix memoir he provides detailed accounts of how Hastings was able to attract and persuade investors as a function of his past successes[1] which had made not only Hastings but numerous investors and venture capitalists very wealthy. Hastings and his story were simply much more valuable to the company and its ability to leverage investment capital. Hastings was a better protagonist and narrator.

The previous quotes from Hastings and Randolph, unsurprisingly, frame Netflix's origins as a good tech based idea to solve an inconvenient problem. Through new models of distribution and a restructuring of the movie-rental process, the company could save user's time, money, and energy by providing a logistically superior, *delivered-to-you* service. Notably each quote diverges from the first and its focus upon distribution, as the second highlights the idea of a gym-style subscription payment model (which wasn't introduced until introduced in 1999), and the last is a wholly different account from co-founder and former CEO Marc Randolph. Randolph's quote, however, seeks to expose the rhetorical work Hastings's stories perform, further exemplifying and exposing the narratorial role of the CEO, who mobilizes the credibility of this title to strengthen different aspects of a company and its lore in varying contexts. Randolph's "side of the story" and his motivations for offering an alternative origin story[2] speak precisely to the importance of affect, drama, relationality, and narrativity in the high-flying worlds of these executives, venture capitalists, angel investors, and technologists. Belief in certain narratives over others results in specific mobilizations and organizations of capital in the order of billions.

With the benefit of hindsight, we can see how Netflix's origin stories perform a fundamental function of investor lore: narratively framing a scalable, potentially profitable idea. One can't help but think of Silicon Valley's unbearably trite yet deeply internalized mantra to "make the world a better place." However, the desperate if not obsessive attempts of the tech industry to brand itself as a positive and altruistic force betray its deeper, financializing motivations of return on investment, by any means necessary. We should not be surprised by these histories however revisionist they may be, but rather should keep in mind that the very basis of the Netflix brand has always been to find and deliver the perfect story at the perfect time to a perfect audience. No one should be better at executing such a task than the CEO.

These stories exemplify the production of the Netflix brand, and the persisting value of the company's Silicon Valley roots. Since its inception, user convenience remains a central theme within Netflix's discourse of innovating movie-rental distribution and home entertainment. Through the feat of logistics management, the company capitalized upon the existing infrastructure of the U.S. mail service, the arrival of DVD technology, and the growing presence of personal computers to "solve": the *inconveniences* of late fees, the multiple trips to the movie store, perusing of the aisles, the possibility of your desired film being already rented out by an earlier bird, and so on.

> The ordering process had to be easy; it could not take more steps to choose a DVD online than to pick up a movie from a store and return it. Randolph was acutely aware of the importance of engaging consumers' emotions, and he wanted the site to be a personal experience, as if each customer opened the door to find an online video store created just for him or her. (Keating 2012, 51–52)

Conceptualized as a hybridization of Amazon and Blockbuster, the founders wanted to provide an explicitly online, direct-to-consumer experience (Keating 2012, 25). As mentioned above: *easy, engaging, and personal.* This quote outlines the centrality of user convenience and experience in the very conception of Netflix and its disruptive model. Keating's history of Netflix outlines the joint expertise of Hastings's background in computer science and Randolph's marketing experience, working with a small team of programmers and marketers to design a user-friendly experience. It is hard to imagine that Netflix could have emerged out of anywhere but

Silicon Valley in the mid- to late 1990s. This is no mistake. The company capitalized upon and actively supported the growth of DVD technologies and home computing/internet technologies in the media ecosystem of the late 1990s. NetFlix.com—in a moment when ".com" carried an unparalleled aura of value—performatively branded itself as a disruptive, cutting edge company providing a superior movie-rental service through these emerging technologies.

> "NetFlix.com has shown itself to be an innovator by taking advantage of the 'mail-ability' of DVD to launch an online DVD rental business that was never possible with VHS," said Tom Adams, President, Adams Media Research. Now, with its "no due date" Marquee program, the company has the potential to revolutionize the DVD rental market that we estimate will grow explosively to over $1 billion by 2002. (Netflix 1999)

> Reed Hastings [. . .] saw a way to combine Americans' love of movies with their love of not getting off the sofa even to go to the video store. (Sauer 2005)

Netflix has always been a proponent of media convergence from the outset, collaborating with numerous tech and entertainment companies such as Toshiba, HP, and 20th Century Fox. Indeed much of Netflix's long-term strategy hinged upon their faith in such teleologies of media convergence, branded as *innovation*. This strategy sought to encourage the convergence of these industries and the growth of DVD within the media ecosystem of the day. Indeed the growth of DVD could not have been more central to the Netflix project, as the mailability of movies in disc format was *the* critical logistic factor in the company's disruption of the Blockbuster rental model. The following press releases evidence some of the company's earliest investor lore, projecting (to) a market of tech-savvy users with home computers who were also likely to be early adopters of DVD, a technology barely three years old in 1998.

> "SCOTTS VALLEY, Calif.,—NetFlix.com is delighted to partner with Toshiba and further increase momentum for DVD rentals" said Netflix president and CEO Marc B. Randolph. "Now every purchaser of a Toshiba DVD player can take advantage of the world's largest collection of DVDs, all of which are available for rent or for sale at Netflix." (Netflix 1998a)

> "SCOTTS VALLEY, Calif., (August 11 1998) [. . .] NetFlix.com is pleased to welcome Twentieth Century Fox to the fast-growing ranks of Open DVD supporters," said Netflix president and CEO Marc B. Randolph. "We are proud to add Twentieth Century Fox's DVD titles to the world's largest collection of DVDs, all of which are available for rent or for sale at Netflix." (Netflix 1998b)

The nearly identical copywriting of these Toshiba and Twentieth Century Fox statements, featuring then CEO Randolph, signals a precise discursive strategy, almost a catch phrase, emphasizing and framing the importance of both tech and entertainment companies as fellow "collaborators" in bringing forth the value of media convergence to the user, but also to these companies and markets. Here Netflix positions itself as a collaborator and champion of DVD as a convergent medium of tech and entertainment; offering its users the opportunity to get a head start on the next major home video technology through the Netflix experience. Early iterations of Netflix's promissory discourses of plentitude and participation are evident here, boasting "the world's largest collection" of titles accessed interactively through the growing medium of the internet.

> PALO ALTO, Calif., June 30 1998—Hewlett-Packard Company today announced a promotion whereby purchasers of HP Pavilion PCs with DVD-ROM drives can rent three DVDs for free. The promotion is co-sponsored by Netflix (www.netflix.com). HP Pavilion PC customers can rent the DVD movies of their choice from the Netflix inventory of more than 1,400 DVD films. Current owners of HP Pavilion PCs with DVD-ROM drives also are eligible to participate in the promotion. "This promotion enables us to help HP Pavilion PC owners experience DVD to the fullest," said Chris Pedersen, worldwide brand manager for HP's Home Products Division. "By providing our customers with simple and convenient access to DVD movies, we are helping them discover what this exciting new medium has to offer." (Netflix 1998c)

This statement from Netflix, quoting an HP executive, further indicates the collaboration Netflix sought to harness with top computing companies to help spread the gospel of DVD, as well as the potential of the computer screen as a new site for film and television viewing. As Marieke Jenner writes about television as a convergence medium—where VCRs, game consoles, and DVDs alter and expand the uses of television screens—this introduction of the DVD-capable personal computer signals a deeper, more multiplicitous level of convergence. At this point in time, for the first time, a user could order a DVD from Netflix and watch it on the same device, foreshadowing the transition to streaming which further collapses browsing, selection, and viewing into an instantaneous process, located within the same window of a web page or application on a single device of virtually every screen size imaginable. In relation to Benjamin Burroughs' idea that digital lore emerges in times of transition, we can see how Netflix's early discourses seek to capitalize on the media hype and buzz of both home computing and DVD as new digital formats which could revolutionize the home entertainment industry, inserting itself as a key player in the emerging markets brought forth by convergence

(2018, 4). This aspect of the Netflix brand has remained constant throughout its history, abiding by and contributing to the Silicon Valley ideology and discourse that constant, never-ceasing technological innovation will inspire and sustain consumption and *use*. Here the growth logic of late capitalism, again, simply re-branded as "innovation," is made more palatable by the alternative and multiplicitous forms of novel "value" it generates for users. The motifs of convenience, efficiency, "free"-time, enjoyment, and quality home entertainment experiences, all justify and legitimize innovation beyond or in spite of market-creating and value-generating motives. As the following chapters show, Netflix's investor lore has always hinged upon such ideologies of innovation applied first to distributing stories, and now to producing them. The setting of the company's investor lore is thus one of a world in constant transition, which is constantly braved by the savvy, risk-taking protagonist, challenging the unknown and turning it into progress.

> About NetFlix: NetFlix is a personalized movie portal where people go to find the movies they would most love. Unique to NetFlix is Cinematch—a technology which compares an individual's movie tastes with those of other like-minded NetFlix visitors and makes highly personalized recommendations. NetFlix currently specializes in DVD movies and offers a revolutionary Unlimited Movie-Rental program for $19.95 per month. NetFlix has raised over $50m in venture capital, ships over 100,000 movies per week, and has partnerships with the leading DVD player manufacturers including Sony, Toshiba, Panasonic, RCA/Thomson, and others. (Netflix 2000)

This "about" section from an early 2000 press release exemplifies Netflix's self-positioning and branding as a collaborative, cutting edge, convergent company. The statement also emphasizes its new personalization software, alongside the scale of its operations and funding. This succinct summary is a rhetorical message for readers as potential investors, signaling the company's aggressive growth strategy, faith in the expansion of DVD, and technological prowess. Notably, these "about" sections, which conclude every press release, have always been updated regularly (at times weekly), providing distilled, rhetorical snapshots of the company's discursive emphasis at a given moment. Highlighting new tech features as well as boasting about ever-increasing numbers of subscribers and available titles, the constant updating of these definitions works to frame Netflix as a dynamic, innovative, ever growing, and thus *investment-worthy*, company. Once more rhetorical promises of plentitude, personalization, and participation (Tryon 2015) present in this "About Netflix" statement signal the importance and ability to attract the attention and capital of not only users but early investors in pre-public offering rounds of fundraising. This was true in the early days of Netflix, and remains so today, as users provide revenue and data, and investors provide financial capital in good faith that it will help improve and expand the company's service to attract more users, and thus more revenue and data, and so on. From the outset, these press releases and "about" sections showcase Netflix's early investor lore as a discourse which projected the myriad potentialities of value this company offered in the late nineties as DVD emerged as the new dominant format for home video entertainment. As a privately owned start-up, the communication of such potential, as well as the citation of a considerable sum of venture capital funding, is a rhetorical call for more investment, angling toward a public offering and thus big returns on early investment. During these early years such discourses were crucial to scaling rounds of venture capital. Indeed just two months after the above statement, Netflix raised another $50 million in a series E funding round, matching the combined total of the three previous years (Crunchbase 2019).

As Keating outlines in *Netflixed*, the company was poised and structured to go public in 2000, seeking to source considerable fundraising, around $75 million, from this offering (2012). The company officially filed for registration with the Securities and Exchange Commission (SEC) on April 18, 2000, precisely as the ".com" bubble burst with the NASDAQ dropping a staggering 25 percent that very week (Randolph 2019, 339). Netflix and its underwriting bank Deutsche, withdrew the registration a few months later in July as the tech stock crash rendered the offering unattractive and unfeasible.

With $57 million in losses, and considerable instability on Wall Street, Netflix approached rental video rival Blockbuster with an acquisition proposition (Keating 2012). Netflix's offer of $50 million is now, well, the stuff of *lore*, as the company's executives were all but laughed out of Blockbuster's head office that fateful September day in 2000.[3] Over the years innumerable articles have been penned by tech, finance, and entertainment trade writers salivating at the misfortune of Blockbuster (which filed for bankruptcy in 2010), each of which somehow manage to reference David and Goliath, with an overall tone of "who's laughing now!" (Fiegerman 2018; Keating 2012; Randolph 2019; GQ 2019). The Netflix-Blockbuster story, which the coming chapters will return to, is one of the most salient teleological narratives of "disruption" we have today, as it is cleaner and more dramatic than say Airbnb or Uber because it is framed cleanly as one small brand unthinkably defeating and replacing the dominant monopoly brand—start-up fantasy 101. Such articles retroactively mock the foolishness of Blockbuster's missed opportunity and (conveniently) praise Netflix's tenacity and continued innovation. Here we can see how history is not only written by winners but also *for* them. This is investor lore work: an infamously American underdog narrative of perseverance and revenge which would eventually lend Netflix and its disruptive lore great credibility in felling *the* rental giant Blockbuster.

In the "post-bubble" world, Netflix struggled to source fundraising and as it grew, and "customer acquisition costs" were adding up at alarming and unsustainable rates. The company cut as much labor as it could (a third of its employees) in efforts to tighten its balance sheets to firstly: budget for a path to profitability at one million users, and second: make themselves attractive to investors in the new financing landscape of 2000/2001 (Keating 2012; Randolph 2019). Randolph's memoir speaks of the difficulty of this cutthroat restructuring, but also of how it refocused the team to the task at hand: "surviving."

By late 2001 Netflix had developed the logistical capability of next-day delivery (for the majority of Americans) through optimizing the circulation of DVDs so users were mailing the discs to localized checkpoints, rather than huge warehouses, for turnarounds which were shorter in both distance and time waiting (Randolph 2019). One step closer to instantaneity. The company also used its proprietary software *CineMatch* to recommend less popular films, and thus effectively reduce demand on new releases. At this time, the company's total accumulated deficit had climbed to approximately $141 million, and it was again time for Netflix to go public to raise the funds they needed to continue, and of course for the early investors, VCs, and money lenders to finally get paid (Netflix 2002).

> Since Merrill Lynch, the lead bank in the consortium that was taking us public, had committed to selling more than $70 million worth of stock on opening day, they weren't going to leave anything to chance. So in the two weeks leading up to the IPO, they had put together a tightly choreographed "road show" that covered all the major financial markets. Like a Broadway production of Miss Saigon opening in New Haven before hitting the Big Apple, the road show began far from Wall Street and ended in New York. Starting in San Francisco, in front of tech-friendly investors, the chartered jet had made stops in Los Angeles, Denver, Dallas, Chicago, and Boston before finally landing for two days in New York City. At each stop, Barry and Reed had been rushed from office to office, conference room to conference room, breakfast meeting to lunch presentation, cycling through all the reasons Netflix was a compelling investment.
>
> —Marc Randolph (2019, 450)

The promotional performance of the roadshow, a joint venture of underwriting financial institution and the top executives of a company, speaks volumes to the affective, relational, narrative nature of financial discourse. Such pre-IPO roadshows are highly performative, designed to create buzz, interest, and *desire* for investment firms and investors to "get in early" on the future action. As Daniel Faltesek notes in his book *Selling Social Media*: "Selling a new security to the public is theater, and the roadshow is an integral part of the performance. Investors buy the dream, not the reality" (2018, 16).

This symbolic journey from San Francisco, heart of the technology industry, to Wall Street, heart of global finance, spotlights the marriage of the two industries in contemporary capitalism, forged by emergent (digital) fantasies of *scale*. Profitability timelines have been greatly extended, and spending costs greatly increased, as long as revenues, operations, and *use* continue upon trajectories upward and rightward. Most importantly, a narrative of future profitability in the tech world must *inspire risk* by capitalizing upon market domination and sheer scale. With Amazon paving the way for tech companies to re-imagine such temporalities and scales of value and profitability—losing $2.3 billion in its first 17 quarters as a public company, but now reeling in *$3 billion in profit per quarter*—Netflix sought to harness a similar temporal logic, by putting forth their own narrative toward market expansion and eventual profitability (Griswold 2019).

Information about Netflix's roadshow is difficult to find outside the accounts of Randolph and Keating. Access to the various drafts of Netflix's S-1 filings,however allows us to imagine what such pitches must have emphasized: 600,000 subscribers, 11,500 titles, $19.95 monthly subscriptions, no late fees, one- to two-day delivery, DVD and internet adoption growing steadily, and cinematch personalized recommendation technology. All plot points suggesting a huge potential market and thus eventual profitability at scale. Randolph's previous quote is helpful in that it highlights how the roadshow—like a theatre production—needs a number of soft openings on the road to Wall Street. These "pitches" are highly dialectical, as the executives and salespeople test various rhetorical strategies, and attentively assess which strategies, which *stories*, excite their audience, as well as which stories inspire fear and skepticism. To put it another way, what visions of the future can be offered to compel as much investment as possible? This facet of investor lore relies upon the affective pull of investment as a risk/reward akin to gambling, buttressed by a socio-professional "fear of missing out." With accelerated financialization and inflation, billions in losses or cash burn, and years (if not decades) of operations can eventually have huge payouts for pre-IPO investors, *even if* an IPO flops (see Uber) early investors can still get paid. The higher the stakes, the greater the reward, and depending on the timing of your investing and selling, impossibly high returns.

THE S-1: TAKE TWO, OR THREE, OR FIVE

On March 6, 2002, Netflix filed an S-1 form with the SEC for the second time, having withdrawn its original registration during the .com crash of

2001. Legally, the S-1 form is the SEC's required document for registering a public company to be traded on national stock exchanges. Such documents are highly symbolic corporate texts which mark a company's transition from start-up to stock, as Hasting's high school graduation metaphor above makes abundantly clear. The S-1 is a highly performative text, and a financial "speech act" of investor lore which betrays many insights into a company's operations, strategies, and philosophies, as the legal function of the document is to thoroughly inform investors of the use of capital, as well as the myriad risks, challenges, and competition the company faces (Faltesek 2018, 21). The nature of the S-1 filing process is dialectical, editorial, and as obvious as it might be to say, *textual*. A company submits an initial filing to the SEC which, like an authoritative editor or reviewer, closely reads the document/manuscript and demands revisions and amendments.

This process often requires multiple drafts, and in this case, Netflix filed five more amended versions (S-1/A's) before the SEC Netflix's filing was deemed legally acceptable. Not(ic)able changes between Netflix's first S-1 and fifth S-1/A include reductions in the size and scale of the home entertainment market in 2001, as $32 billion in domestic consumer spending was revised to $29, video rental and sale was changed from 80 percent to 78 percent of this market at totals of $21 billion, not $23. The final S-1/A also disclosed Netflix's cashflow upfront on the first summary page, and on summary sections throughout the document to clarify the companies 2001 revenues of $75.9M, net loss of $38.6M, and total accumulated deficit of $141.8M. The "proposed maximum aggregate offering price"—the maximum amount an IPO can potentially raise—was also meaningfully reduced from a starting point of $115M to $94.875M, which would in the end yield an actuality of 5.5 million shares sold at $15.00, raising $82.5M, $5.775M of which would go to the underwriter Merrill Lynch. Similar to any sort of sale price negotiation, companies—and their underwriting firms—strategically set "placeholder numbers" for such "proposed maximum offering prices" in efforts to frame the size of the IPO they hope to yield. Results of course vary due to the varying factors of the market, and the *feelings* of investors and "the market" from the day of a company's IPO, and for the rest of that company's public life.

Reading Netflix's S-1's alongside various other investor lore texts (press releases, executive interviews, letters to investors, quarterly and annual reports, keynote speeches, and so on) provides a broader picture of Netflix's value narratives. The risks layed out in the S-1 are counterbalanced by these other texts where executives highlight the company's ability to *overcome* such risks and challenges in its market, and more importantly to investors, to generate profit and thus eventual returns on investment.

Netflix's 2002 S-1 is chock-full of numbers touting the speed and scale at which DVD was expanding in the home entertainment industry, and how Netflix was riding the momentum of this technological tide change. For example, the document cites the firm Adams Media Research multiple times, framing the then-current status of the market: "Domestic consumers spent more than $29 billion on in-home filmed entertainment" in 2001, and projecting: "The number of U.S. households with a DVD player will grow to 69 million in 2006, representing approximately 62 percent of U.S. television households in 2006" (Netflix 2002, 1). Scale scale scale. Chuck Tryon's thesis that the Netflix brand is sustained by promises of plentitude, prestige, participation, and personalization hold true even in Netflix's earliest years (2015, 106). Such promises are emphasized in the summary, as the document attributes Netflix's growth to its "unrivaled selection" of 11,500 DVD titles, growing participation and early adoption of Netflix's DVD rental experience—2.8 percent market penetration in the Bay Area—and of course its proprietary personalization software *CineMatch* which creates a "customized store" for each user. Bringing these selling points from press releases and private investor pitches to Wall Street signaled the company's desire or perhaps more accurately necessity for capital and expansion. The strategy of start-up to IPO here evinces yet again the increasing entanglements and interdependencies of Silicon Valley and Wall Street, as the tech industry increasingly encourages mass spending and debt financing in hopes of either acquisition or going public. High tech, high risk, high reward.

The fifteen-page *Risk Factors* section of the Netflix S-1 details the challenges of the company's business model, and the various factors which may "adversely affect our business" or result in the loss of "all or part of your investment." This section is organized by dozens of bold statements, with brief paragraphs explaining each specific risk. The rhetorical style of this section of the S-1 reads like an Investor FAQ resource, designed to anticipate skepticism and guide the potential investor with an algorithmic logic of "if . . . then." Yes these are the risks, but each risk is also an opportunity. The document repeats its confident, distilled "summary" at the beginning of multiple sections throughout, and other sections such as "Growth Strategy" seek to showcase *how* Netflix will overcome these and capitalize upon these risky "ifs." The structure of the risk factor section explains each aspect of Netflix's operations, and its plans maintain operations and turn them into value. However, the purpose of the S-1 of course is to legally inform the investor of the risk they are willingly taking on. Implicit in this framing is the promissory contract of purchasing stock, and the affective, gamblified pull of investment. In spite of 121 pages of legal business rhetoric and financial data, everyone knows the world of finance is fickle and unstable, and such uncertainty is what provides the thrill of value accumulation made meaningful by the potential of *loss*. Such waves of feeling and discourse indeed sustain the perpetual movements of the market. In this context, the early investor is always already deeply invested in the skepticism and *dis*belief of other early investing actors, which would provide not only the personal and financial satisfaction of the successful performative (speech) act of investment but also the ability of that investor to potentially buy more shares at lower rates should they feel so inclined. Finance itself is in many ways a de facto media—now screen—industry of world-making. To reiterate my thesis again, the greater investor lore is at mobilizing investment capital, the easier it is for a company to realize its performative promises, futures, and worlds.

The Risk Factor section is ordered to discuss the company's expectation of continued operational losses, ability to continue to grow and satisfy the user base, ability to maintain its technological infrastructure, ability to maintain its logistical operations, ability to maintain its DVD library and favorable contracts with studios and distributors, uncertain future internet privacy and policy conditions, and even the long-expected mega-earthquake expected along the West Coast's San Andreas fault is mentioned as potential risk to the company's Bay Area headquarters. The motifs, or "growth strategies," are placed throughout the S-1 serve to assuage the fears of risk, and are recognizable as the staples of the Netflix brand: (1) maintaining high user value propositions, (2) full faith in the continued growth of the technological ecosystems of DVD and the internet—including potential future digital delivery, (3) its ability to continue to work with studios and distributors to promote DVD and share DVD revenues (and potential digital delivery rights), and (4) its ability to compete with other home entertainment; with the S-1 citing HBO, Blockbuster, Walmart, Amazon, Hollywood Entertainment (video rental), and Best Buy.

As the coming chapters will examine, Netflix's brand maintains this foundational continuity of technological ecosystem growth (now smart, mobile, and platform TV), technological development and "innovation," plentitude and personalization (now to the level of producing content for increasingly niche audiences), and of competitive advantage evinced by the erasure of Hollywood Entertainment and Blockbuster as rental services and its relative dominance in streaming video. In other words, Netflix's executives have been successful in showing investors how it is still dedicated to the same mission, and has positioned itself over time to continue to deliver that mission amid vast changes in the convergent screen industries of tech, finance, and culture.

What this (lengthy) prologue to Netflix's initial public offering establishes, is the critical maneuvers and performances of Netflix and its investors in the five years it took the company to become *NFLX*. This is the stage upon which the ensuing drama(s) of Netflix have been played; the necessary steps it has taken to arrive on Wall Street and participate in global finance's unparalleled opportunities to access and mobilize the great sums of capital required to keep expanding at scale. The following seasons of Netflix are defined in many ways by its status as a publicly traded company and the attendant legal and communicative responsibilities that entails. The coming chapters thus examine the shift and expansion of Netflix's investor lore as the company and its executives were no longer only seeking private support, but were now also seeking to raise and leverage capital through the stock market as an operational financial tool.

DVD AND GOLIATH

I think everyone recognizes that an IPO is like high school graduation, it's big at the time but with hindsight it's really only a beginning of something else.

—Reed Hastings, May 23, 2002.

On May 22, 2002, Netflix successfully made its initial public offering, selling 5.5 million shares at $15 each, raising $82.5 million in the process, and closing its first day of trading up 12 percent. By the end of the year, the company also doubled its revenue from 2001, and boasted $15 million in positive free cash flow. These were the first steps toward "making good" on its promises made to investors by proving the value of its model (Netflix 2002). Going public importantly brought with it important new forms, genres, and volumes of investor lore from Netflix in the form of quarterly and annual reports, as well as other investor relations materials. This first ever Netflix 10-K annual report features a cover page image of a couple cast in the warm glow of the TV, relaxing on the couch, remote in hand, with opened Netflix DVD envelopes prominently displayed on the coffee table also hosting a bowl of popcorn.

This idealized, if not cliché, image of a "movie night in" yet again solidifies the centrality of user convenience and experience in Netflix's investor lore, signaling that the decades-old practice of film viewing at home now carries new potentialities of value for the consumer and, therefore, the investor through the emergent DVD market and Netflix's novel distribution/ rental model. The following page in this report features the stylized brand logo of the company's name and a brief description set against a bold red background. This is importantly followed by the first-ever shareholder letter from CEO Reed Hastings, highlighting the company's annual performance, business model, potential value, and strategy for the future.

Fellow Shareholders. I'm pleased to report to you that 2002 was a truly remarkable year for Netflix. In this, our first year as a public company, we met or exceeded all of the financial and operational goals we had set for ourselves 12 months earlier. During a time of continuing uncertainty in the technology and

financial markets, we were one of only eight technology companies to successfully complete an initial public offering in 2002. And in each of our three
subsequent reporting periods as a public company, we outperformed investor
expectations for key financial metrics, including revenues, expenses, EBITDA,
and free cash flow.

—CEO Reed Hastings (Netflix Annual Report 2002)

Alluding to the plummeting of tech stocks in the dot com crash, Hastings
boldly positions Netflix as a truly exceptional technology company, thriving
and expanding in such uncertain times and unstable markets. The letter outlines how Netflix's business model had continued to strengthen its brand in
the emergent DVD rental market, focusing on Netflix's proprietary personalization software in the section titled "merchandising magic," and the Netflix
consumer experience in the following section "entertainment: convenience,
selection, and value." Highlighting the increased adoption of DVD and home
computing, Hastings argued and assumed that as these media ecosystems
continued to grow, so too would Netflix.

After an optimistic sign off projecting the potential (growth) of the coming year, Hastings includes the following postscript message, seemingly as a
reward to whoever the reader may be for reading:

P.S. If you're not already a Netflix subscriber and would like to try out our
service at no obligation, I would like to personally invite you to take advantage
of a free, extended-trial offer at netflix.com. Simply type in 60177346 in the
promotional code field, and enjoy Netflix for free, with my compliments.

—CEO Reed Hastings (Netflix Annual Report 2002)

While free trials were nothing new at this time, this particular example
anticipates the now ubiquitous e-commerce freemium-subscription model, in
which a digital service or product is provided for free, either indefinitely or
for a given period of time, in efforts to promote a premium service or product
to be in essence *rented* from the platform. Here we can see from the outset
the importance of subscriber growth, and the value this brings to the company
in terms of potential subscription fees, but also consumer trends and word of
mouth publicity, even if the user doesn't end up subscribing after the trial.
In many ways, Netflix still operates upon such a logic, balancing free trials,
tiered subscription plans, and varying cost structures to optimize the complex
ratios of revenue, usage, and data which fuel the machine of the platform.

Subsequent annual reports maintain and reinforce the themes of Netflix's
early investor lore, emphasizing scaled growth in terms of revenue, subscriber
base, and library size. This projected confidence in the continued expansion
of DVD and internet ecosystems and importantly the company's logistical

capability to manage their combination of these two media technologies. The 2003 report features informational paragraphs with titles such as "the intelligence behind the brand," "our customers tell the story," "our numbers are growing," and "rich content, more choices" found on every other page, signposting an overarching narrative of superior user convenience, experience, and value reinforced by relevant quotes from users:

> In my opinion, this is a truly great program. It has everything: gigantic selection, ease of use, shipping timeliness, and low cost. I recommend it to all my friends.
>
> —C.S., Warwick, RI (Netflix 2003, 6).

> Netflix knows me better than I know myself. It picks movies for me that I never would have chosen, and I've loved almost every one of them. (C.B., Fairfeild, CA [Netflix 2003, 8])

These selected quotes seem nearly too good to be true, performing the important rhetorical function for the reader to affirm, repeat, and reinforce the brand messaging, business model, and strategy of Netflix in layman's terms of value. Such testimonials boast of the user experience of the service, website, catalogue, shipping, and proprietary recommendation software, each of which is framed as interrelated form of user value. In the context of an annual report and 10-K filing, these quotes speak to the potential financialization of user-audiences and their experiences of Netflix. Indeed Hastings signs off his letter to investors by thanking "shareholders and happy customers alike" for their encouragement and support in making 2003 a great year for the company, positioning both the financiers and the users as privileged early adopters and investors (Netflix 2003, 9).

The above quotes come from anonymous users outside Providence and San Francisco, with other similar comments coming from Naperville (suburban Chicago) and Pearland (suburban Houston), citing proximity to major metropolitan areas, but importantly projecting an image of an idealized, suburban, middle-class user (not far off from how Hastings frames himself in Netflix's origin stories). The motif of the mailbox throughout the reports of these early years also reinforces this message, often showcasing collaged arrays of mailboxes alongside a similar collage of faces; the message being as unique as you and your mailbox may be, Netflix has everything for you.

BLUE'S GOT MAIL

In the DVD era of Netflix, its 2004 annual report stands out as an important one for a few reasons. As Gina Keating has outlined in her vividly detailed and dramatic corporate history of Netflix *(Netflixed)*, this year marked the entrance of Blockbuster and Wal-Mart into the DVD-rental-by-mail market, alongside an impending threat from Amazon to do the same (2012). Here the risk posed by Blockbuster and Walmart, and the buzz of Amazon entering the market sent the Netflix stock into a volatile tailspin, crashing from a first-quarter high of $39.77 to a fourth-quarter low of $9.25 (Netflix 2004). In the narrative arc of the stock NFLX, this would constitute the rising action of the second act; igniting the drama of competition and uncertainty inherent to the market.

Responding to such a crisis required, more than ever, new *lore* from Netflix; an aggressive discourse of confidence and reassurance for all stakeholders: users, investors, employees, and executives. The key messages which emerged from this crisis were first, that Netflix remained the dominant leader in "the marketplace we invented . . . providing the best online entertainment experience" (Netflix 2004, 3), and second, that the entrance of these competitors would instigate a positive feedback loop of overall market growth and consumer awareness *of* this new market, which would translate into more overall subscribers.

The aggressive entry of *Blockbuster Online* into the market also instigated a price war, coming in at $19.99/month for three DVD rentals at a time, two dollars below Netflix's $21.99 price point, from which Netflix dropped to $17.99, and Blockbuster to $17.49 (Keating 2012). Despite maintaining a user base of 2.6 \ million by the end of 2004, Netflix was forced to alter its pricing model yet again in fear of losing subscribers.

> 2004 was also a year in which we demonstrated our willingness to make hard choices—including lowering prices and deferring profitability—to protect our market leadership. We believe market share leadership is key to long-term category leadership [. . .]. Our superior product, brand strength, and deep operational experience give us what we believe are the highest gross margin and the lowest operating costs in our business [. . .] attributes that strengthen our confidence in our ability to prevail over the competition.
>
> —CEO Reed Hastings (2004, Netflix, 9).

Such rhetoric is a positive framing of a potentially existential threat. Hastings' use of the term "category leadership" also indicates the shifting logics and temporalities of value brought forth by platform capitalism, as maintaining a less profitable but growing market share of users was argued to be strategically advantageous and valuable in the long run. This signals the complex reworking of media value in the age of digital convergence, wherein growth trumps profit, and can be sustained by the new flows of financial capital, investment, and debt into the tech industry. Amazon is a contemporaneous example of a company operating on the same model, foregoing profit and returns to instead aggressively re-invest all possible revenues in its own expansion and market domination (Khan 2016, 711). With the benefit of hindsight, the new economic rationality of financialization is abundantly clear here, as early investor-adopters of Netflix or Amazon with the patience and faith to stay the course were rewarded with stocks appreciating into the tens if not hundreds of thousands of percentage points. As Khan cunningly outlines in her Yale Law Journal article *Amazon's Antitrust Paradox*, both legal and cultural systems of belief in a profit-first, "consumer benefit" economic rationality has been fundamentally circumvented and abused in our late information age. Today's flows of global financial capital—accelerated by increasingly networked global information infrastructures—now afford for this emergent "Californian" ideology and techno-liberal rationality of speculative fiction: growth, market dominance, and massive returns for the investing few.

As video rental migrated to the internet, it developed new forms of user "engagement" through profiles, ratings, and social networking, each of which generated new forms of user data central to Netflix's operations, from macro-scale logistical management to its individualizing promise of personalization. This design of such proprietary technologies and infrastructures for new flows of media mobilized not only new circulations of data, content, and capital but also a new language through which to communicate the value of such properties and practices; the value of user data. The message to users being: "participate, tell your friends, rate our films, help us help you, *engage.*" The message to investors is much the same: "participate, tell your friends, buy (more) stock, help us help you, *engage.*"

This new language of the value of user data for the video rental industry was heightened in the 2004 annual report amid the challenges and uncertainty brought forth by competition and the subsequent volatility of the company's stock, as Netflix sought to reassure investors of its superiority and resilience. Framing their technological prowess as both a competitive advantage and differentiator from the competition was imperative to this annual report, and Netflix's plans for the future. In the face of uncertainty, the message communicated in this report was that Netflix had the information, *the data*, to weather the storm, innovate its way out of it, and all the while continuing to grow.

Headers on the pages of Hastings' letter to investors boasted of the steadily growing scale of Netflix's operations: "3 million subscribers," "35,000 titles," and "525 million ratings." Such statistics clearly sought to impress and reassure shareholders that the company's categorization, recommendation, and logistical technologies and infrastructures would ultimately guide and deliver users (away from Blockbuster) to Netflix, and keep them coming back (Netflix 2004, 1, 6, 4). Alternating graphic pages featured photoshopped film stills of Mike Myers's Austin Powers, E.T., and Frankenstein, each posed with the iconic red Netflix envelopes, accompanied by footers which also boasted the intricacy of Netflix's user data in the form of fun facts:

> Mike Myers is Austin Powers in Goldmember. Other Austin Powers movies available through Netflix: "International Man of Mystery" and "The Spy Who Shagged Me" Netflix carries 18 other Mike Myers titles and more than 50 other titles from the Saturday Night Live Alumni. (Netflix 2004, 4)

> E.T. the Extra-Terrestrial is the fourth highest grossing film of all time, with $453 million in theatrical revenue. The other top five films are also all available through Netflix: Titanic (1), Star Wars Episode IV (2), Shrek 2 (3), and Star Wars Episode I (5). But Netflix's top renting title, Mystic River, only grossed $90 million in U.S. theatrical revenue. (Netflix 2004, 8)

These data, supported by playful graphics, furthermore showcase the efficiency of the Netflix platform to gather and process data at scale, turning these patterns of user behavior into added value for the user. "Unlimited" user choice, convenience, personalized recommendations, and claims to social capital signaled potential growth and thus future value throughout this report. Industry lore emerges most poignantly in times of heightened uncertainty and transition, the same is true of investor lore, perhaps even more so (Burroughs 2015; Curtin, Holt, and Sanson 2013). The challenges of 2004 brought forth an increased attention to the *value of data* in concert with Netflix's proprietary recommendation software and logistics and distribution infrastructures. This emphasis was specifically counterpointed to the brick-and-mortar store model of Blockbuster, and in fear of a platform with eerily similar advantages: Amazon. Netflix had a head start as *the* tech company doing video rental, and it needed to keep it.

Expanding this emphasis upon the value of innovation and the company's technological soul, another notable discourse—or plot point—re-emerged in the 2004 report: Netflix's expectation to provide "internet delivery of movies" from the Netflix website itself in the following year. While digital delivery was briefly mentioned in the company's S-1, Netflix and its executives now felt confident, or perhaps desperate, enough to reintroduce the idea to investors in 2004, as a provocative image of a future Netflix. Prefiguring the now ubiquitous metaphor of "streaming," Hastings stated in his letter a hopeful belief in the market potential of this new mode of distribution, with his company positioned as a Silicon Valley tech firm with three million relatively tech-savvy, online users, familiar with their website interface (Netflix 2004 10). Contextually, Netflix was clearly still comparing itself to the old world retail goliath Blockbuster, who had made brief efforts in testing digital delivery in 2000 with Enron TV set-top boxes, some of which caught fire in users homes, right before the Enron company *itself* caught fire, mired in controversy as criminally fraudulent accounting practices were revealed, and the company's stock crashed from $90.75 to $0.26 in just over a year (Segal 2020).[4]

Other set-top boxes and video-on-demand technologies slowly but surely emerged throughout the early 2000s, and Netflix was keenly aware of how this would affect their business, and how such offerings could heighten competition in the home entertainment market. Netflix's projection of "internet delivery–coming soon" once more signals the solutionist ideology of the tech industry and Netflix's lore, in which the problems of increasing competition and limitations of physical media could be solved through innovation, further convenience, and greater speed. It also contributes to the broader teleology of American consumer technologies, accelerating and miniaturizing at all costs; betraying deeply internalized desires to save any modicum of space or time in daily life. The logical succession to the logistical rationality which allowed Netflix to grow as a DVD-rental-by mail-company is the ultimate just-in-time flexibility of instantaneity. While this may be taken for granted today, streaming was still a powerful and just out of reach idea in mainstream consumer technological environments of the early 2000s, making the market potential of instant delivery ripe for investment. Netflix and its executives thus sought to convince investors through various means of communication that it was the best positioned company to capture this market.

Subsequent annual reports elaborated further upon Netflix's "alternative video delivery" plans, using the language of "downloading" in 2005 and then "instant delivery" in 2006:

> We are absolutely focused on positioning Netflix to lead this market. It's important to remember that downloading is just another way to deliver content, an alternative to the mail, or the local video store, or to cable, or to satellite delivery. The winners in downloading will be the companies that provide the best content and the best consumer experience, and that's what we do best. With millions of online subscribers addicted to the Netflix Website, we will have both a mass audience and the most compelling consumer experience in the market, which will give us critical advantages as we begin to offer downloading as a second delivery option.
>
> —CEO Reed Hastings (Netflix 2005 Annual Report, 8)

> There is a growing array of services offering Internet delivery of movies, [. . .] our strategy for achieving online movie-rental leadership is to continue to aggressively grow our DVD subscription business and to transition these subscribers to Internet video delivery as part of their Netflix subscription offering.

To begin that transition, in January 2007 we introduced our "instant viewing" feature that enables subscribers to watch movies on their PCs.

—CEO Reed Hastings (Netflix 2006 Annual Report, 3)

On top of the existing threat posed by Blockbuster's aggressively advertised online subscription service, 2006 brought with it the entrance of Amazon and Apple's iTunes store as competitors in the new realm of movie download rentals, referenced but not named at the beginning of the second quote above. Within this context Hastings emphasizes both the scale Netflix's user base and its unique user experience as critical advantages in the increasingly competitive movie-rental landscape. Netflix's dominant discourses of user convenience and experience are clearly displayed here in both quotes, by explaining the *value* Netflix's experience of downloading and instant viewing (streaming) will bring to the user. The industrial race this signals, as stated above, was a complex and convergent challenge of securing a broad catalogue of content and finding/creating the best mode of delivery: digital and on-demand. The beginnings of this "transition" is a marked moment in Netflix's story; the precipice of a large-scale leap in this media ecosystem toward the digital infrastructures of the internet: home computing, faster broadband, more efficient file compression and delivery; and away from the logistical infrastructures of DVD—distribution centers, roads, postal services, and physical discs. The rising action of Act I came in the forms of increasing competition in intertwining DVD rental and internet delivery markets, heightening the risk and uncertainty of survival, and sparking a race into uncharted territory. In the words of the chief executive narrator himself "Because DVD is not a hundred-year format, people wonder what Netflix's second act will be" (Helft 2007).

NOTES

1. Pure Software's successful IPO, merger with Atria, and eventual acquisition by Rational Software were three major financial prizes for Hastings and the investors who believed in him from the beginning.

2. See Randolph's 2019 book *That Will Never Work: The Birth of Netflix and the Amazing Life of an Idea*, as well as Gina Keating's *Netflixed: The Epic Battle for America's Eyeballs* (2012) for more dramatic and detailed accounts of Netflix's origins.

3. See Keating and Randolph for detailed accounts of this moment in Netflix's history.

4. Enron filed for bankruptcy just a year after signing a (twenty-year) VOD contract with Blockbuster.

Act II

Hope *Streams* Eternal (2007–2011)

SCREEN PASTURES

Each year since we invented online DVD rental in 1999, Netflix has focused on understanding the preferences of our subscribers and on improving the customer experience. And each year the result has been rapid growth in subscribers, revenue and—since we went public in 2002—earnings [. . .]. Our leadership in online DVD rental provides a powerful platform upon which to build leadership in Internet delivery of video rental. As with any innovation, it will take some time for Internet delivery to emerge as a significant business. With limited content available for Internet delivery for the foreseeable future, we believe our ability to offer our large and growing subscriber base a full range of rental content at one low cost, delivered either by mail or streamed over the Internet, gives us a great advantage over any stand-alone Internet delivery service.

—CEO Reed Hastings (Netflix 2007 Annual Report, 2)

The line "we invented online DVD rental" in the Hastings quote above emerged as a motif in Netflix's lore during this period, framing the company not only as an innovator and creator of technology but also importantly *of markets*. Hastings makes an appeal to his credibility here, as this self-positioning as an expert with the experience to lead and "innovate" the online future of film and television home entertainment. The implicit message being "we created and now dominate online-DVD-rental-by mail, and will do the same for streaming." It is precisely at this time that the key terms *platform* and *streaming* emerged in Netflix's investor lore. Notably the metaphor of the "stream" had only been used to characterize flows of revenue or popularity of a cultural or technological product, the main*stream*, prior to 2007 in

Netflix's investor relations materials and public communications. The expansion of this metaphor to include a new content delivery protocol speaks to the convergence of Netflix, and platform capitalism more generally, not only in relation to industrial practice but also importantly also language and its new multiplicities, mobilizations, and monetizations of meaning and metaphor. Conceptualizing and communicating the value of streaming to Netflix's user "preferences" and "experiences," the introduction of these terms in relation to Netflix's long term vision performatively projected the strategic shift to digital delivery as both an innovation and an inevitable future which Netflix would dominate. Acknowledging the time such innovation takes for widespread adoption and profitability, Hastings reassures the reader that the company's dual offering of DVD and streaming is an advantage in both the near and the far terms, again for both users *and thus* investors.

Fluctuating temporalities of financial value—such as investment, risk, debt, growth, and returns—were brought forth by the new temporalities of user value, convenience and experience which the *instantaneity* of streaming provided. The collapse of Netflix's browsing interface into a viewing interface removed even the trip from the computer to the mailbox. The "watch instantly" tab signaled Netflix's adaptation within these specific technological and economic landscapes, and the emergence of another complex and convergent media ecosystem: streaming. The now technologically and culturally ubiquitous term *streaming* was introduced in Netflix's 2007 annual report, and the company has in many ways delivered its performative promises of streaming through its platform model. In retrospect we can now see how the strategic shift to streaming accelerated the company's capability to further mine behavioral user data regarding watching habits and taste formation, yet the language surrounding data is notably vague within Netflix's investor communications during this transition, especially in the early years of streaming. While this may not be surprising to read now, it is nonetheless important to examine the rhetorical emphases of Netflix's investor lore at this time to examine how the transition to streaming was and continues to be communicated, justified, and sustained as a valuable industrial practice.

Gina Keating's *Netflixed: The Battle for America's Eyeballs* describes the era in which Netflix introduced streaming (2006/2007) as "High Noon."[1] Threats came from multiple sides, with Blockbuster's integrated in-store/online offering directly leaching subscriber growth from Netflix, as well as studio supported download-to-own models from Amazon, iTunes, and Wal-Mart, and lastly RedBox kiosks, all attempting to capture a percentage of the film and television rental market (2012). Such competition from alternative DVD rental and digital video delivery services put pressure on Netflix's discursive promises of value and superiority, as the company's subscriber growth and stock value began to fall in tandem (Keating 2012, 397; Netflix

2007). Reiterating that online-DVD-rental was indeed *its invention,* Netflix consistently sought to reassure investors of its leadership and competitive advantage as an innovator. Streaming thus represented a future market which Netflix would invent and dominate once more. However, at the height of this "standoff," Netflix was seriously hemorrhaging subscribers—and thus revenue and shareholder earnings—to Blockbuster's in-store and online coupling: Blockbuster Total Access[2]. In a massive stroke of luck for Netflix however, the falling out between Blockbuster CEO John Antioco and finance magnate and majority shareholder Carl Icahn, led to Antioco leaving Blockbuster. Antioco was replaced by Jim Keyes—a firm believer in brick-and-mortar retail—who, in Keating's telling, ran Total Access and eventually the company in its entirety, into the ground, precisely as Netflix migrated online (Keating 2012, 389). With the breathing room this good fortune allowed, Netflix began to return to its previous rates of growth and market dominance, focusing upon expanding the reach of its platform beyond the screen of the computer monitor to the TV.

During the week of Monday January 15, 2007, Netflix launched its streaming feature. At this time Hastings deflected questions about competition from Blockbuster to foreshadow his vision of the coming entertainment platform wars from the likes of YouTube and gaming:

> "I worry mostly about the competition for time—user-generated videos, online games," Hastings said, adding that for now the live service is not expected to add to Netflix revenues. "We've held our own on rentals, we'll nail this too." This will eventually include "a user model, an economic model and a membership model, growing film selection and screen selection. . . . We'd love to have this on cellphone screens, computer screens and televisions connected to the Internet."
>
> —CEO Reed Hastings (quoted in Hardy, January 16 2007)

The growth of streaming also brought challenges similar to the company's early years: fostering the adoption of new technologies and securing content to deliver. However, this time around the company had the massive backing of millions of subscribers and investors, and importantly the revenue streams that came with them. Harkening back to Netflix's DVD ecosystem growth strategy from the late 1990s and early 2000s, the transition to streaming employed similar underlying strategies but with the profound shift from fostering a new physical media format (DVD) to an increasingly digital and computational entertainment landscape. Since the beginnings of Netflix's lore of internet delivery, Hastings made clear his desire to get streaming from the PC to the TV and beyond, as the quote above evidences. Supporting and capitalizing upon developments in broadband internet speed and the growing ubiquity of home computing, Netflix—at heart a tech company—sought to broadly expand the convenience of the user experience it provided through partnering again with major tech companies and entertainment conglomerates. The project this time being to get Netflix's platform infrastructure onto as many devices and screens as possible, beginning with the computer, and moving quickly to the television and its appendages: the DVD player, gaming consoles, set-top boxes, and digital video recorders (DVRs).

The narrative of value projected here was again one of the mutual benefits of convergence, as these consumer electronics *and* content companies were in the business of getting their respective TV compatible hardware devices or cultural products into people's homes. Netflix thus offered its services to streamline both industry objectives simultaneously. The story Netflix told its partners was that the value of these consumer electronics, as well as that of licensed movies and shows, could then be heightened by the addition of Netflix's platform software and its accompanying millions of users / audience members. However, beneath this idea of corporate "collaboration" and mutual benefit, the integration of Netflix into these devices was also a Trojan Horse of sorts in the battle for attention Hastings mentioned above. While consumers may have been more likely to purchase a device such as a Netflix compatible DVD player, game console, or smart TV because of its streaming capability, the flows of user time, attention, and now data, were beginning to be channeled—indeed *streamed*—away from DVD sales and rentals, gaming, and linear television to Netflix's platform, thus redirecting revenue in these economies of attention, and industries of leisure. This is the second, discursively obscured, edge of Netflix's strategy of industrial convergence, present primarily in its hardware partnerships:

"Watching movies at home will never be the same. Netflix on Xbox 360 is an entertainment first, and we are bringing friends together with the best in entertainment content like no other device in the living room," said John Schappert, corporate vice president of Interactive Entertainment LIVE, Software and Services Business at Microsoft. "We are creating a completely new social entertainment experience, and Xbox 360 will be the only video game system where you can access your library of instantly streamable movies from Netflix and turn any room into a virtual movie theater." (Netflix 2008a)

"Consumers crave compelling and immediate content, and the Netflix online streaming movie feature can provide instant gratification. This alliance underscores LG's goal of developing smart technologies that deliver flexibility, convenience and control to consumers," said KI Kwon, President of the Consumer Electronics Division of LG Electronics USA, Inc. (Netflix 2008b)

Through the executives of Microsoft, LG, and other consumer electronic producers, Netflix allied these narrators to help proliferate the motif of collaboration and convergence within its investor lore. Echoing the ecosystem growth strategy of DVD, the above press releases indicate how such partnerships "redefined" the domestic entertainment space of the living room through providing "flexibility, convenience, and control." Accelerated by the increasing speed of internet infrastructures, immediacy and instantaneity were importantly added to Netflix's discourses of superior user convenience and experience: *adding user value.* This language was and still is important in supporting and advancing these central elements of Netflix's investor lore and brand identity.

The discourses of value related to consumer choice, control, and trust in the brand were also importantly situated against the backdrop of the Great Recession. Instead of the costly trip of taking the family to the movies, the message here was rather that Netflix "brings the theater to you." The emerging streaming ecosystem and economy, in classic platform capitalist form, relied upon the externalization of infrastructural costs onto the user such as broadband connections, smart TVs, gaming consoles, set-top/streaming boxes, or other streaming compatible consumer devices. Netflix's introduction of the streaming feature relied upon making these externalized sunk consumer costs invisible, allowing the company to boast the extremely low price points of $4.99 and $7.99 streaming-only options, integral to its narrative of affordability and consumer choice.

Partnerships on the tech side included LG, Xbox (Microsoft), Playstation (Sony), Samsung and others. This also included the launch of Roku, a streaming tech company incubated at Netflix's Silicon Valley HQ, whose primary product was the Roku Netflix Player. This set-top box fostered the convergence of computing and supplementary televisual technologies to get (the) TV online (Netflix 2008). In the early days of streaming, such innovations advanced Netflix's overarching themes of flexibility, convenience, choice, and innovation. The message was that streaming heightened each of these aspects of user value, but it was ultimately still your choice as a user as to whether Netflix's DVD or streaming "experience" was best for you and your home entertainment needs or wants for now.

On the content side, Netflix courted Starz, NBC, CBS, Disney-ABC, Starz, and EPIX among others for digital rights to stream their content. At the dawn of the streaming age, Netflix was able to negotiate licensing deals in which media conglomerates and content companies vastly underestimated the value of the digital rights of their content and were oblivious to the latent *wealth* of behavioral data such content contained (Curtin et al. 2014; Keating 2012; Nocera 2016). Through its streaming platform *designed* to extract user data, Netflix was able to harvest crucial and increasingly intricate audience data as a new form of value, all the while projecting these licensing deals as a win on all sides: greater choice for users, additional revenue for content owners, higher sales of Netflix compatible devices, more subscribers for Netflix, and as always, potential returns for investors. However, user data was intentionally not yet a part of any public conversation at this point. The following two quotes from an October 2008 press release showcase precisely this point, with quotes from Netflix and Starz executives:

> "The coupling of Starz Play with our growing library of streaming content is an important step forward for both companies and for consumer choice," said Ted Sarandos, chief content officer for Netflix. "Our deal reflects the creative ways we are working with content partners to expand the profile and the number of choices our subscribers can watch instantly over the Internet, in addition to the 100,000 titles we offer on DVD through the mail."

> Starz Entertainment president and chief operating officer, Bill Myers, noted that this agreement marks a significant step forward in Starz' efforts to provide consumers with choice and convenience so that they can watch Starz programming wherever and whenever they want. "Netflix has grown to be an innovative leader in the home video space and we are delighted to offer their customers our unique and robust collection of movies on a subscription basis. This agreement is a strong vehicle to promote the Starz brand and showcase Starz' leadership position in the premium movie category." (Netflix 2008c)

These press releases seek to maintain and reaffirm Netflix's promise of plentitude (aka consumer choice) within the emergent streaming market, alongside the convenience and flexibility of the instant viewing feature of the platform (Tryon 2015, 104). Leveraging the added value of their digital distribution infrastructure to older content, Netflix relied upon their ability to sell this idea to Starz, among other major film and television studios, networks, and conglomerates as both a reality and a red herring in the early years of the transition to streaming. By this I mean that streaming did provide new revenues, audiences, and infrastructures for content owners, but at a cost to overall DVD sales and rentals. The latent value of streaming data extracted through this platform distribution model, however, remained unseen by these content owners. With the successes of the company's first and second acts—going public and continuing to grow the DVD ecosystem and rental-by-mail model—Netflix was able to draw upon its history for both the rhetorical capital such investor lore carried, arguing that they would be able to also achieve similar success by fostering the growth of the emerging technological ecosystem of streaming.

SEEING RED

Drawing some similarities to the dot com crash which Netflix had survived and made its IPO, the company also boasted its ability to weather the dire economic landscape of 2007/2008:

> Netflix ended 2008 with 9.4 million subscribers, up 25 percent from a year earlier, and fully diluted earnings per share of $1.32, up 36 percent from the prior year. That's solid performance, particularly in the challenging and uncertain economic environment we faced in the second half of 2008 [. . .] Our results make it clear that consumers find our service compelling. We combine a superior value proposition with an outstanding customer experience, and we continuously improve our product offering through investments in our Web site, content, distribution, and customer care.
>
> —CEO Reed Hastings (Netflix Annual Report 2008, 1)

Netflix's use of the phrase "superior value proposition" emerged in 2008, and would become a motif signifying the theme of consumer choice throughout its lore in the years to come. Projecting a corporate commitment to such consumer choice through Netflix's range of plans, from $4.99 to $16.99 a month, such messaging was clearly meant not only as a more affordable alternative to going to the movies but importantly also as a shot at an inflating pay TV market where the average monthly cable plan was around $50 (Netflix 2008; McAlone 2016). Framing this user entertainment *value proposition* in relation to subscriber and revenue growth, this quote argues that Netflix's dual offering of DVD and streaming resonated with users in such a "challenging and uncertain economic environment." Netflix continued to push their narrative of offering a superior, convenient, and affordable home entertainment experience at a better price through the clever innovations and efficiencies of convergence and disruption. With Blockbuster recently vanquished and streaming on the rise, Netflix had the technological prowess and the pricing power to offer such a range of subscription plans.

Preaching the gospel of convenience and affordability through the self-righteous narrative of "consumer choice," we also now know how Netflix forwent the maximization of immediate profitability in favor of growing its market share and user base. Evidencing platform capitalism's new temporalities of value—debt, scaled growth, public offering, profit, earnings—Netflix has kept prices as artificially low as possible for as long as possible in efforts to grow the market share/user base to continue to extract, collect, and process as much behavioral *data* rather than as much capital as possible from their users. Expanding its targets and taking aim at all online entertainment and linear pay TV, the emergence of streaming represented a pivot from shipping the discrete units of DVDs to an expansive digital offering of content. This shift from physical circulation of rentals to online *access of content* is now taken for granted, but is nonetheless still crucial, as it indicates a capitalist fantasy of seemingly infinite expansion and the supposed bottomless well of data extraction that digitality has come to represent. The crucial investment here is in the narrative of almost limitless digital *scalability:* of users, of use, of data, and of content, always in service of potential future value.

Streaming as an alternative distribution model was integral to Netflix's new strategy, as it began to license seasons of television which users could consume wholesale, without having to ship multiple disc sets around the country. The opportunity to scale the digital consumption of content—seasons of TV as opposed to hours of movies—in this way cannot be understated, but for the company at this time, it presented a delicate situation in which they needed to communicate to users and investors this new *use(r) value*, while not alarming the cable studios and networks they were licensing such content from.

> Netflix streaming has become a valuable additional profit stream for content owners. Some content owners fear that licensing to Netflix will undercut other, larger profit streams. The Starz example suggests otherwise. We have carried Starz since October 2008 and we have not licensed HBO. Over that time, Starz' Multichannel Video Programming Distributor (MVPD) subscriber count has grown, and HBO's has not. At a more granular level, the Starz Original "Spartacus" was available at the same time on Netflix as on MVPD, and it was a big success in MVPD viewing, as shown by its Nielsen ratings. Even the DVD box sets have been a great success. So having content on Netflix does not appear to materially harm the revenue of that content on other channels. In other words, the evidence is pretty clear that content that is also licensed to Netflix generates more money for its owners than content that is withheld from Netflix.
>
> —CEO Reed Hastings & CFO David Wells (Netflix 2010a,
> Q4 Letter to Shareholders, January 26, [2011], 6)

Projecting the capitalist mantra "a rising tide lifts all boats" Hastings' quarterly letter, now coauthored by CFO David Wells, sought to reassure stakeholders that Netflix posed no threat to legacy film and television industries. The above quote even goes as far as to claim that content-owning media conglomerates would be missing out on the opportunity to harness the added *value* that streaming on Netflix provides in terms of revenue, cultural awareness, and brand/title recognition for that content. While *Spartacus* was indeed a "granular," if not exceptional, example, Netflix relied upon such messaging as content owners were becoming increasingly wary of Netflix's user growth—and stock value—with the rise of streaming as an increasingly popular alternative to linear cable and premium television offerings. The provocative narrative of Netflix's increasingly powerful position was taken up by both popular and trade publications during this era. During this time, DVD sales and linear TV subscriptions began to decline, with such phenomena largely attributed to Netflix and the rapid growth of streaming (Arango 2010; Copeland 2010; Orlin 2010). Major *media* companies were outraged that a self-identifying *tech* company was biting into what they perceived to be *their* margins. Netflix's insistent industrial identification as a tech company was highly strategic and allowed the company to get a foot in the door by projecting myriad forms of added value, while sowing the seeds of "disruption" and long term competition in other markets. As Ramon Lobato has pointed out in his work, Netflix, like Facebook and Uber, mobilizes an industrial (over)identification as a tech platform (rather than media, advertising, or transportation services) to circumvent industrial norms, policy regulations, and importantly competition (2019). This is a major factor in the discursive work of disruption. We must rethink and expand industry lore to examine the shifting, conflictual, and convergent nature of *media industries*, considering specifically those actors which strategically and rhetorically place themselves "outside" the industries and markets they seek to disrupt. Again, investor lore allows for a more multiplicitous and multiperspectival approach to researching the slippery objects of platforms, and these polymorphous and often misdirecting processes of platformization.

THE STREAM ENGINE

For the past year, executives at big media companies have watched Netflix with growing resentment—for its success in delivering movies and television shows via the Internet, for its stock price nearly quadrupling, for its chief executive being named businessperson of the year by Fortune magazine. (Arango 2010)

Yes, you heard this before. The Death of Cable TV. Yet, it hasn't happened. But now, so many disruptions are happening in the video space, cable TV is really stepping towards the cliff. Don't expect the cable industry to just give up. We'll get some new insights next week when the largest U.S. cable operator (23 million cable customers), Comcast, reports its Q3 earnings and subscriber count. Comcast cable customers dropped nearly 3% in Q2 compared to last year. In Q2 for the industry overall, a record 711,000 subscribers abandoned cable TV, and six of eight operators suffered their worst quarterly subscriber losses ever. (Orlin 2010)

With the doubling of Netflix's stock value in fiscal 2010, alongside Forbes magazine naming Hastings businessperson of the year, the legitimacy and influence of the Netflix CEO's vision and voice also grew. With Hastings as the brand figurehead, the company's image was further elevated as a rising star on Wall Street and in Silicon Valley, and an increasing threat in Hollywood, specifically to the TV industry. Alongside this increased attention and scaled growth, Netflix began featuring full length investor letters to shareholders every quarter, with the Q4 letter often functioning as an annual review. The increased volume and detail of the now quarterly letters signaled the increasing necessity and opportunity of Netflix's investor lore for the company as it grew, helping investors and stakeholders understand and navigate Netflix's reasoning and development as streaming began to subsume DVD. The accelerated rhythm and volume of these investor relations documents, and the stories they tell, discursively capitalized upon the positive trends in subscription rates and revenue, frequently citing comparative year-over-year (Y/Y) growth percentages and figures in the millions to display and heighten the rhetorical purchase of such data (see table 2.1). In a similar vein, transcripts of quarterly investor relations earnings calls also appeared on the Netflix investor relations blog in 2010. Highlighting selected questions from financial analysts, answered by Netflix's executives. These interviews provided more information, lore, and "evidence" in a relational format for investors to pour over. Here the narratorial role of the company's executives is evident, as their confidence and authority in the face of investor questioning either further entrenches the reader in the narrative of their lore, or causes them to question the reliability of the narrator.

Midway through 2010, Netflix's streaming service began to overtake DVD rentals, and the company also expanded into its first international market: Canada.

"Q3 represents our fourth consecutive quarter of more than one million net subscriber additions. This growth is clearly driven by the strength of our streaming offering. In fact, by every measure, we are now primarily a streaming company that also offers DVD-by-mail," said Reed Hastings, Netflix co-founder and CEO. "At the same time, the introduction of our streaming offering in Canada in late September has provided us with very encouraging signs regarding the potential for the Netflix service internationally." (Netflix 2010, Q3 Letter to Shareholders, October 20; 1)

Table 2.1 Netflix's Q4 2010 Earnings Data (Netflix 2011)

(in millions except per share data)	Q4 08	Q1 09	Q2 09	Q3 09	Q4 09	Q1 10	Q2 10	Q3 10	Q4 10
Net Subscriber Additions	0.72	0.92	0.29	0.51	1.16	1.70	1.03	1.93	3.08
Y/Y Change (%)	59	20	72	95	61	85	255	278	166
Subscribers	9.39	10.31	10.60	11.11	12.27	13.97	15.00	16.93	20.01
Y/Y Change (%)	26	25	26	28	31	35	42	52	63
Revenue ($)	360	394	409	423	445	494	520	553	596
Y/Y Change (%)	19	21	21	24	24	25	27	31	34
Operating Income ($)	38	36	53	49	53	58	77	70	78
Y/Y Change (%)	87	138	54	45	39	61	45	43	47
Net Income ($)	23	22	32	30	31	32	44	38	47
Y/Y Change (%)	45	68	22	48	35	45	38	27	52
EPS ($)	0.38	0.37	0.54	0.52	0.56	0.59	0.80	0.70	0.87
Y/Y Change (%)	65	76	29	58	47	59	48	35	55
Free Cash Flow	51	15	26	26	30	38	34	8	51
Buyback ($)	10	43	73	130	79	108	45	57	—
Shares (FD)	60	61	60	58	55	55	54	54	54

Our three virtuous cycles of subscriber growth are: 1. More subscribers means more money to license content with, which drives more subscriber growth. 2. More subscribers means more word-of-mouth from subscribers to those who are not yet subscribers, which drives more subscriber growth. 3. More subscribers means we can increase R&D spend to improve our user experience, which drives more subscriber growth. You can see the power of these virtuous cycles in our marketing spend in Q4: we spent about 10% fewer dollars in marketing than one year ago, yet subscribers grew 63% over the last year.

—CEO Reed Hastings & CFO David Wells
(Netflix 2011, Q4 2010 Letter to Shareholders, January 26, 1; 2)

This operational *and rhetorical* tide change from DVD rental to streaming offered evidence of Hastings' long-promised transition of the company's subscriber base in precisely such a direction. Lauded for his company's initial disruption of Blockbuster, Hastings was now praised for "cannibalizing" the company's own DVD market by "disrupting his own business before it gets disrupted" (Copeland 2010). The passages above introduce this report with a focus on net subscriber additions ("net ads"), a sustained emphasis within the company's investor lore. The repetitive and cyclical rhetoric of increasing subscriber growth demonstrates the layered financializability of the user. User subscription revenue is re-invested into content and technology spending to improve the user experience, thus mobilizing social and cultural capital associated with entertainment value among existing and potential users. All of these forms of financial, social, and cultural capital are thus re-invested into the platform through browsing, viewing, consuming, rating, analyzing, and discussing *Netflix* in any capacity. As Netflix externalizes infrastructural costs onto the user (screen devices, TV appendages, internet plans, etc.), we can see here how it also externalizes or "optimizes" marketing costs through word of mouth enticed by the provocative power of the brand. The "underdog" identity of tech start-ups—even when they've grown into multi-billion-dollar companies—often remains in the culture of the company as a "disruptor," lending it significant rhetorical and narratological purchase first in the form of novelty, and second a warped pathology of an entrepreneurial spirit fighting "against the odds," "against big industry," and all the while "making the world a better place." On multiple scales, from users having a new "experience" of TV, to vacation rental, or car-sharing, investors jockey to get in early on the next major shift in x industry. The culture of Silicon Valley relies upon some degree of provocation or controversy as a means of drawing attention and belief in its narratives. At the end of the day platforms are brands too; however, not all publicity is good publicity, as the highly impressionable "hand of the market" (investing class) makes abundantly clear.

As an increasingly popular vehicle of film and television distribution, the expanded *user experience* of streaming on Netflix became an essential aspect of the company's brand.[3] The quote above, however, suggests oversimplified positive feedback loops of revenue, investment, and word-of-mouth promotion. Framing subscriber value simply as sources of revenue and brand advocacy importantly omits the trove of behavioral data that users represent. Guiding public focus away from data here and throughout this era was strategic, as it was and remains Netflix's greatest competitive and operational advantage.

Riding the momentum of growth in the late aughts, Netflix's streaming lore reiterates its central narrative that *user value in terms of experience translates to the potentiality of shareholder value over time. Time.* The change here is thus not the brand message, but rather an emergent narrative of the new temporalities and scales of value, for the user's experience, and, therefore, the shareholder. Netflix's euphoric growth and increased valuation throughout 2010 was championed as proof of the exponential scalability and disruption of digital platforms. As accelerated and digitized practices of viewing and consuming *narrative fiction* correlated with accelerated and digitized processes of financial *capital* accumulation; a new form of fictitious capital seemed to be emerging. Through ardent faith in a future of ubiquitous computing (necessary for streaming), Netflix's increasing success in 2010 seemed to signal the realization of the company's performative investor lore: bringing into being user value and shareholder value in tandem.

HOUSE OF (CREDIT) CARDS

Emboldened by the successes of 2010, Netflix's investor lore shifted to aggressively focus on expanding its streaming content catalogue and recommendation technologies under the overarching goals of brand strengthening and as always, subscriber growth. On March 15, 2011, the news broke that Netflix had outbid both HBO and AMC for the exclusive rights to the American remake of the British political thriller *House of Cards*, from director David Fincher, featuring Kevin Spacey. Careful to avoid the threatening rhetoric of "production," Netflix executives spoke at this time rather of "exclusive rights" and "licensing":

Hi, Ted Sarandos, Netflix Chief Content Officer here. We're delighted to tell you that in late 2012 Netflix will be bringing to our members in the U.S. and Canada exclusively "House of Cards," the much-anticipated television series and political thriller from Executive Producer David Fincher and starring Kevin Spacey. We've committed to at least 26 episodes of the serialized drama, which is based on a BBC mini-series from the 1990s that's been a favorite of Netflix members. [. . .] The TV shows and movies that you are able to watch instantly are licensed from movie studios, TV networks, distributors and sometimes directly from the producers of the films and TV shows. "House of Cards" is unique, as it is the first exclusive TV series to originate on Netflix. Typically, we license TV shows the season after they run on a broadcast network or cable channel and occasionally, we have episodes from a current season [. . .] In all of these cases, the shows are produced before we bring them to Netflix. "House of Cards" represents a slightly more risky approach; while we aren't producing the show and don't own it, we are agreeing to license it before it is successfully produced. We've found the gripping, serialized one-hour drama, such as "Heroes," "Lost," "Dexter" and "Weeds," has become a very important part of the Netflix experience and over the years, we've been able to add these shows from many different channels, with the notable exception of HBO. With David Fincher's unique vision, the incredible acting skills of Oscar winner Kevin Spacey, and a great and timeless story of power, corruption and lies, we think "House of Cards" will become a big hit among Netflix members and thus, represents a manageable risk.

—CCO Ted Sarandos
(Netflix Media Blog 2011, March 17)

I quote this company blog post at length because it contains and foreshadows the emerging investor lore of Netflix's fourth act: the era of "global" original production. Just two days after the news broke through entertainment industry publications *Deadline* and *The Hollywood Reporter*, this post, while shying away from the language of production, marks the entrance of Netflix's discourses of value surrounding the now infamous brand of the "Netflix Original." Here Sarandos displays the company's confidence in its viewership data of the 1990s BBC *House of Cards*, its ability to license 26 hour-long episodes *without* a pilot, and its ability to attract top creative talent. Sarandos also strategically gestures toward the prestige of HBO—whom they famously outbid for this very show. This statement thus frames the risk that *House of Cards* represented for the platform, and emphasizes how the company has strategically positioned itself to turn such risk into *value;* as a hit for users and an exclusive prestige brand for the platform. Walking the line between humility and hubris, this statement extends Netflix's performative promise of plentitude and prestige by showcasing the company's willingness to take risks and directly challenge not only distributors but also would-be producers for content (Tryon 2015). This moment marks a shift in the temporalities of value generation Netflix had been built upon: licensing, recommending, and distributing content with existing audiences, brand associations, and cultural cache. The list of strategic factors cited by Sarandos here all has to do with how the affordances of the *platform* allow the company to effectively *pre-empt, predict,* and *guide* the success of content *before* it is produced. Indicative of the Silicon Valley ethos of disruption, and platform capitalism more generally, the discourse surrounding this shift was that Netflix's platform model generates far more accurate and detailed data than previous industry metrics (Nielsen ratings, focus groups, "gut feelings"[4]). Again, Haven's idea of industry lore is evoked here, but rather than just "the conventional knowledge among industry insiders about what kinds of media culture are and are not possible, and what audiences that culture will and will not attract" (2008), Sarandos' explanation for Netflix's platform model for original content also importantly communicates moreso *investor lore*: the emergent discourses among *investing actors* about what types of *user experiences* are and are not *valuable*, and which *users* those *experiences* will and will not *engage*. Foreshadowing the emergence of a new type of industry lore, this statement speaks not *directly* of data, algorithms, or stock value, but rather simply implies that the viewing history of the 1990s series, the talent, and the exclusivity of this content on Netflix will provide an exciting experience and thus add affective value to many existing and potential users.

Perhaps downplaying what we now know was the beginnings of a massive strategic and industrial shift, *House of Cards* and the original production conversation shockingly did not come up in the following two quarterly earnings reports and executive Q&A calls. It wouldn't be until Q4's extensive 2011 annual review that House of Cards would come up again in Netflix's investor relations and media center materials. My third chapter elaborates further upon the development, evolution, and negotiation of the provision of original content and the new discourses and circulations of value that came along with this shift, but it is important to acknowledge their emergence here in early 2011.

FALL AND RESPONSE

Of course the euphoria of 2010 was not built to last, and Netflix took an unforeseen and nearly deadly turn later in 2011. This time the challenge was not of a broader economic trend or rising competition, but rather a problem of its own making. As streaming grew rapidly the company sought to divorce its DVD and streaming services into two separate subscription companies, splitting up its $9.99/month dual streaming and DVD plan to individual plans at $7.99/month each; in other words, a 60 percent price increase ($15.98/month) if you wanted to keep both services. Netflix was to become purely streaming, and the DVD branch would become its own company, rebranded later as "*Qwikster,* a Netflix company" (Netflix 2011). The announcement of this divorce initially appeared in a July 12 press release, and the decision was expanded upon at the bottom of the fourth page of the Q2 earnings release on July 25, 2011.

Despite general agreement from Silicon Valley and Wall Street in regard to the economic rationale behind the decision, the announcement sparked swift and widespread user backlash, and a wave of *un*subscription as the price hike approached. Hastings' appeals to this economic rationality were simply too far a field from the brand identity they had so carefully fostered as a "champion of consumer choice" and affordability. What resulted was Netflix's worst quarterly performances up to that point, as the company lost 800,000 subscribers in Q3 with a subsequent stock value descent from an all-time high of $304.79 in July to $62.37 by the end of November (Netflix 10-K 2012).

In the midst of this crisis, Hastings published both a blog post and YouTube video on September 18, 2011, both titled "An explanation and some reflections," in desperate efforts to further communicate Netflix's decision. His apology post frames the problem of the service split as one of a lack of communication:

> I messed up. I owe everyone an explanation. It is clear from the feedback over the past two months that many members felt we lacked respect and humility in the way we announced the separation of DVD and streaming, and the price changes. That was certainly not our intent, and I offer my sincere apology. I'll try to explain how this happened. For the past five years, my greatest fear at Netflix has been that we wouldn't make the leap from success in DVDs to success in streaming. Most companies that are great at something—like AOL dialup or Borders bookstores—do not become great at new things people want (streaming for us) because they are afraid to hurt their initial business. Eventually these companies realize their error of not focusing enough on the new thing, and then the company fights desperately and hopelessly to recover. Companies rarely die from moving too fast, and they frequently die from moving too slowly. When Netflix is evolving rapidly, however, I need to be extra-communicative. This is the key thing I got wrong. Arrogance based upon past success. We have done very well for a long time by steadily improving our service, without doing much CEO communication. Inside Netflix I say, "Actions speak louder than words," and we should just keep improving our service. But now I see that given the huge changes we have been recently making, I should have personally given a full justification to our members of why we are separating DVD and streaming, and charging for both. It wouldn't have changed the price increase, but it would have been the right thing to do.

> —CEO Reed Hastings
> (Netflix Media Blog 2011, September 18)

Ambiguously directed at users and investors ("everyone") the post continues on this line of thought, elaborating upon Hastings' appeals to economic and business rationalizations for the split. Managing to boast of Netflix's successes while still apologizing for the shock of the price increase, Hastings described rapid industrial movement and evolution as the very means of survival in the contemporary business world. Importantly this signaled the company's deeply held Silicon Valley ideology, and perhaps anxiety, of perpetual innovation. Doubling down on the decision, Hastings' elaborated upon the increasingly divergent underlying cost structures of streaming and DVD-by-mail, as said costs were quickly changing in both content licensing and commercial shipping. The potential digital economies of scale that streaming represented were being hindered by DVD, and Netflix sought to cut streaming loose from this restraint. For Hastings the message was that along the road there were going to be some growing pains, but at the end of the day growth would still be growth, and *streaming—not DVD*—was the only future for such potential. Rhetorically aligning himself with the user, Hastings goes on to state "Many members love our DVD service, as I do, because nearly every movie ever made is published on DVD [. . .] I also love our streaming service, because it is integrated into my TV and I can watch any time I want." Communicating the *varied* user values of each service rhetorically framed Hastings' argument and justification for separating the services.

> We feel we need to focus on rapid improvement as streaming technology and the market evolve, without having to maintain compatibility with our DVD by mail service. So we realized that streaming and DVD by mail are becoming two quite different businesses, with very different cost structures, different benefits that need to be marketed differently, and we need to let each grow and operate independently. It's hard for me to write this after over 10 years of mailing DVDs with pride, but we think it is necessary and best: In a few weeks, we will rename our DVD by mail service to "Qwikster."
>
> —CEO Reed Hastings
> (Netflix Blog post 2011, September 18)

In the related YouTube video hyperlinked at the end of the post, Hastings is pictured alongside Andy Rendich, the former head of DVD operations at Netflix, who he introduces as the new CEO of Qwikster, "a Netflix company." In this video Hastings and Rendich both seek to highlight how the divorce of these services will allow each of them to grow and "innovate at great rates." Both the post and this video sought to persuade the reader of the diverging priorities at Netflix, as streaming increasingly represented instantaneity, televisual content, and international expansion, and DVD was domestic, physical, and largely movie-centric. Reading between the lines, the message is ultimately *scalability*. Pure streaming signaled scaled consumption in terms of instantly bingeable television and film (versus physically mailed DVDs), and scaled operational expansion: international markets, users, and content. Despite these last-ditch efforts to justify this decision, the damage was already done. Trade publications and consumers blogs wrote off both the post and the video as awkward, tone-deaf, and virtually meaningless, as necessitating users to juggle separate accounts, billing, and queues alongside the added cost was clearly a user nightmare (Keating 2012). By early October Netflix announced in a terse press release that its DVD service would ultimately be staying at Netflix. The damage to the brand was simply not worth the "optimizing" potential of the split. Nonetheless, the company refused to budge on the $7.99 monthly charge per service, stating that this would intentionally channel new subscribers toward streaming.

I dwell upon the public-relations of this debacle as it indicates the changing nature of what the Netflix brand was coming to represent in the entertainment landscape, and how it was being negotiated by users and investors alike. The investor lore of this moment, Q3 2011, also importantly represents a failed performative, what Austin calls an "infelicity" (1962, 14). The "Qwikster debacle" evidences the wide-reaching rejection from both Netflix's user base *and* investor base of this particular narrative of value which the company tried to sell. Driving home my argument that streaming represents a new financialization of the user, this moment is a fissure in the Netflix narrative, where masses of upset users unsubscribed and helped crash the valuation of the company—wittingly or not—by frightening Wall Street. With subscriber growth being the most important metric for investors to assess and project the value of the new media economics of Netflix's business model, this represents a brief sliver of potentiality for *collective action among users within platform capitalism*.

While this was no doubt primarily a phenomenon of individuals assessing and critiquing the value proposition of Netflix's price hike, this moment nonetheless elucidates the structural dependence of platforms upon their users, and perhaps offers forms of potential collective organization and negotiation. Investors knew that if the *investments* of user data, attention, time, capital, content, information, labor, and sociality ceased to flow, the platform would not be sustainable or thus at all valuable. Each of these value investments users make *in* platforms thus represents a potential for resistance, as they can now be leveraged against the platform in harmful and meaningful ways. The old adage "hit them where it hurts . . . their wallet" now offers a multitude of targets, as the flipside of platform capitalism's expanded and multisited project of financializing every aspect of everyday life offers users the opportunity to again leverage, withhold, and redirect, their increasingly *valuable* datafied behavior as a potentially counteractive or perhaps even creative, generative new politic. While I cannot say that I am overly hopeful for such a "user consciousness" or mobilization, platform capitalism's structural dependencies upon users and their data nonetheless opens up such an immanent fissure of possibility. If the political will could be mustered, redefining all behavioral user data as *the property of the user* would go a long way in resisting the increasingly surveillant and extractive logic of today's digital economies, and could offer forth new organizations and applications of these powerful technologies of measurement and communication.

Exacerbated by the tailspin of the company's stock value, the crisis of cancellations, as well as the approaching end of its Starz content contract, Netflix's Q3 investor letter reinforced the importance of the streaming user experience, the plentitude of its increasingly televisual content library, and the potential of international expansion to its long term vision and valuability.

Youssef Squali (Jefferies & Company—Analyst): Thank you very much. Good afternoon, everybody. Reed, just a couple—really one question going back to the DVD business. Clearly it's—as it starts atrophying, I'm just trying to understand what is the value of that business to you now, outside of just being cash cow, are there any synergies that still exist between that and the streaming business, and if there's any value to actually keeping it under the same umbrella? Thanks.

Reed Hastings : Youssef, at this point it's a source of profits funding our international expansion, and it's a source of satisfaction to the more than 10 million members who subscribe to our DVD service, whether they also subscribe to streaming or not. And so we will keep it and run it steadily, and keep the service. So that would be the plan going forward.

Operator: Thank you. (Operator Instructions) Our next question comes from—

Reed Hastings: That's okay, guys. Our job as we see it is to try to anticipate your questions and answer as many of them proactively in our investor letter as possible. I will take the absence of telephone questions that at least in that dimension, we are doing a good job. We want to thank everyone for their support. We know it's been an extremely challenging time to be a shareholder over the last couple of months. And I want to tell everyone that we are extremely focused on growing our streaming business on a global basis and believe it's a tremendous opportunity to create a very valuable and important and respected firm. And that's what everyday here at Netflix is spent doing. With that, thank you all very much.

Operator: Ladies and gentlemen, thanks for participating in today's program. This concludes the program. You may all disconnect. (Netflix 2011a; 2011 Q3 Earnings Call Transcript, October 24, 2011)

While there is no publicly available audio recording of this quarterly earnings interview, this exchange highlights the lowlight of Netflix's streaming era thus far. The presumed silence on the line following the operator's "Our next question comes from—," which Hastings quickly attempts to spin in favor of the efficacy of his investor letter, suggests a disenchanted investing community, stunned by Netflix's fall from greatness, the shattering of the illusion of the Netflix narrative. The backslide in total number of subscribers, while still at 23.8 million exemplifies a rupture in the speculative and narrative logic of interpolating trends in efforts to predict future value and avoid future risk. This dramatic reaction of Wall Street, with the abrupt halt and brief reversal in Netflix's growth further evidences the highly affective, emotional, and relational nature of finance.

The day after Netflix Q3 earnings release, Forbes technology writer Mark Rogowsky declared:

The damage done to the Netflix story is irreparable. No matter what happens from here, the notion of the stock sitting on a multiple based on hope, endless faith, feverishly loyal customers, a "management premium," a growth premium, etc. is gone—forever. From here, the company is going to be judged significantly more on results. This is a rite of passage in all "story stocks" and it's often painful for investors. And this is painful in the extreme: $305 down to below $100 in just a couple of months as the growth story ends, the multiple gets crushed, the future looks awfully uncertain. (Rogowsky 2011)

Anticipating the hit to the brand, and the accompanying hit to the credibility of the company's investor lore, Netflix continued to emphasize its technological prowess and identity as a forward-looking Silicon Valley firm. Hastings and Wells articulate here the motifs of affordability and "innovation"—with its narrative logic of developing ever better HCI and user experience design—as long term value signifiers and competitive advantages.

While we and our competitors face the constraints imposed by the traditional licensing structure of cable, we have many advantages over linear premium pay networks. We are unbundled, and charge a very low price of $7.99 a month. We are pure on-demand so we can create more compelling user experiences than a primarily linear channel. We are personalized, so each user interface is tailored specifically to the individual taste of a given consumer, helping them to easily

find movies and TV shows they'll enjoy. Finally, we can innovate at Internet
pace rather than cable-set-top-firmware-update pace.

—CEO Reed Hastings & CFO David Wells
(Netflix 2011a, Q3 Letter to Shareholders, October 24, 6)

This focus on "internet pace" innovation is communicated clearly and
importantly by the company's increasing use of the now ubiquitous tech
industry concept and term *user experience* in its investor lore. Beyond customer experience, the exact phrase *"user* experience" and discussions of the
"Netflix experience" rose in the company's investor relations materials and
lore and now pertained almost exclusively to streaming. Hoping to never look
back to the Qwikster mishap, and simply maximize their DVD service profits
for as long as possible, Netflix turned its sights and its lore ever toward the
future; a future it desperately needed to sell. As the presence of the term *experience* increased, it also expanded rhetorically, and discursively to encompass
each element of a user's engagement with the "ever improving" platform,
such as user interface design, personalization, browsing navigation, content
offerings, viewing practices, ratings, recommendation engagement, and
device compatibility. Each of these facets of the user experience represents
the generation and extraction of invaluable user data; guided user behaviors
designed to be monitored ever in efforts to be monetized.

While we now know how these data-generating experiences, more accurately defined as HCIs or perhaps better yet transactions, inform every aspect
of Netflix's design and operations, in the early days of streaming, this knowledge was less common. However, the varying utterances and citations of *user*
experience in Netflix's investor lore sought to persuade investing stakeholders as to its ability to perpetually innovate and improve upon the valuable
experiences of Netflix for *users*; the affectual bond necessary to retain users,
their data, and their subscription revenue. Diverting attention away from the
benefits these mechanisms afforded the company, the narrators of Netflix's
lore focused instead upon the figure of the user, and the motif of innovation
to project a *provision* of value, guiding the conversation away from the company's surveillant extractions of data and value. The above quote elucidates
the rhetorical functionality of how Netflix began to conceptualize, transform,
and ultimately brand practices of film and television viewing as *user experiences*. Beyond just navigating the user interface and browsing the catalogue
on various devices, the act of streaming and watching through Netflix turns
film and television into products of convergence, technology, and platform
capitalism; in other words, into *content*. This language in Netflix's investor
lore was a pivotal discursive development in communicating and selling its
operational expansions into original production and international markets.

The new forms and flows of *value* that can be extracted from user experiences depend entirely upon the (media) industrial convergence of late capitalism producing a ubiquitous platform ecology. For Netflix, this is represented in, and communicated by, the violent cannibalization of the company's DVD service in favor of streaming. In the Q3 2011 earnings call, Hastings innocently states "we think the future is brightest by focusing on streaming" when asked about maintaining the high cost for users who wanted to keep both DVD and streaming services. Translation: the potential speed and scale at which the company could grow its market share and extract value will always be exponentially higher for streaming than it would ever be for DVD. By using pricing power alongside a rhetorical emphasis on the bright and endlessly innovative future of streaming, Netflix sought to guide consumer choice, and investor attention, toward streaming in efforts to offset losses in subscribers and to show investors that the streaming user base would continue to grow. *Scale scale scale.* By promising to both users and investors that streaming would be constantly improving and expanding user experiences of prestige, plentitude, participation, and personalization, Netflix sought to instill and rehabilitate faith from investors in its future (Tryon 2015, 104).

Building upon the now stated prioritization of streaming over DVD, Netflix's investor lore throughout the remainder of 2011 and into 2012 emphasized the increased profitability of domestic streaming, increased growth in international markets, and increased anticipation for original production as a potentially important new strategy. These discursive developments within the context of Netflix's larger narrative of *value* marked another shift in the company's investor lore. The new strategies and new media economics of original production and international expansion would have to be continually and convincingly framed more now than ever before. As the halcyon days of Netflix's "story stock" status were declared dead, financial analysts argued that the company would now have to become a more "results and performance" based stock to ever hope to recover (Rogowsky 2011). This crisis point in the financial/narrative arch of Netflix exemplifies a sort of "test of character" moment for the company, and its figurehead Hastings, whose audience(s) had never been bigger.

To review, the transition to streaming was Netflix's third "act" in which the instantaneity, speed, scale, and perceived immateriality and affordability of this new user experience were championed in the company's investor lore as added *user values*. Citing its role in the fostering of DVD, Netflix drew upon this history to persuade investing actors—users, financiers, shareholders, content owners, employees, and so forth—that it could once again help popularize the new media ecosystem of streaming as a wellspring of potential value. The dawn of streaming allowed for the company to propagate such narrative discourses of value, and for a time also convince content owners that it could bring in extra revenue for old and currently airing content—indicative of the arc of Netflix's transition to from shipping DVD films to streaming TV; from logistics to a pure-play platform. In other words, the matrix of these *values*, which Netflix performatively projected and provided, drove investment and subscriber growth, further suturing the goodwill, faith, and capital of users and investors in this emerging streaming platform economy. Conversely, the Qwikster debacle emphasized a faltering moment of such faith in Netflix *and* its story of value. As droves of users canceled their subscriptions, so too did Wall Street, sparking anxieties about their *subscription* to this platform narrative of value. Cannibalizing its profitable DVD-rental-by-mail user base and taking on short term losses in hopes for long term returns, the transition to streaming represents the platform capitalist fantasy that *hope streams eternal* in its perceived infinitude of content, delivery, extraction, globality, and capitalization. Such a fantasy, however, is only made tenable by users subscribing to these narratives of value, thus providing an immanent collective potential for organization, mobilization, and representation of users, should we truly analyze and critique such stories, and have the courage and will to imagine and build alternatives.

With streaming established and becoming increasingly ubiquitous, the announcement of original production foreshadowed Netflix's fourth act. Beginning in 2011, the question of original programming marked the beginning of Netflix's transition to becoming a self-described "global internet television network." Evidencing the performative nature of investor lore, the narrative of value surrounding original production began to be framed and projected years *before* the release of the first "Netflix Original," which is contested in and of itself.[5] This begs the question, what exactly constitutes a "Netflix Original"? Exclusive licensing? First window distribution? Studio production? Global rights? The Netflix "N"? The next chapter thus excavates how the strategic shift to "originals" necessitated new narratives, negotiations, and projections of value. After the Qwikster mishap devastated the company's stock, and licensing costs and competition were steeply increasing, original programming and re-emphasized global expansion emerged as the narrative discourses of value, the *lore*, which would recover and sustain the company's fantasy of perpetual growth and ultimately reward the investing actors who stayed the course.

NOTES

1. For more on the story of the Netflix—Blockbuster competition, see Chapter 12 *High Noon* of Keating's *Netflixed: The Battle for America's Eyeballs (2012)*.

2. "Blockbuster Total Access" was the company's strategic bundling of in-store DVD rental and DVD-by-mail in a subscription package with no late fees.

3. Analyses of the emergent sociocultural practice of *binging* are abundant, alongside phrases such as "Netflix and Chill," "What's on Netflix," and "Want to go watch Netflix?" entering the popular vernacular alongside the growth of streaming. See Jenner 2015; 2016; McCracken 2014; Tryon 2015, Wayne 2017).

4. Todd Gitlin's 1983 book *Inside Prime Time* is a foundational text for the concept of industry lore, and examines the "gut feelings," "scuttlebutt," and "intuition" of TV executives and producers during this era.

5. While *House of Cards* (2013–2018) is lauded as the company's flagship original, the company's Norwegian co-production *Lilyhammer* (2012–2015) was the first show distributed exclusively by Netflix (outside Norway) a year before *House of Cards*, and is thus by some measures and accounts the first *actual* Netflix Original.

Act III

Networking the "Global Original" (2011–)

STUDIO SYSTEMS ENGINEERING

After establishing streaming not only as a feature of the Netflix experience but rather its future, Netflix's third and ongoing act has been its twin expansions into both international markets and original content provision. These directions were, however, strategically obscured and revealed for various reasons throughout the Netflix story, as this chapter will outline and exemplify.

> David Miller (Caris & Company): Reed, against the backdrop of other distribution services bidding up for the content in the streaming window, what is your feeling about either acquiring an equity interest in the studio or, at the very least, starting one yourself? With creative financing, you could produce script-driven content on your own at very little cost relative to the size of your P&L.

> Reed Hastings: David, generally, I'm a believer in circles of competence and it's really easy for companies, as they grow, to step out of that. And, in particular, when we start taking creative risks, that is reading a script—that is, reading a script and guessing if it was going to be a big hit and who might be good to cast in it—it's not something that fundamentally as a tech company or a company run by a tech CEO like myself is likely to build a distinctive organizational competence in. We think that we're better off on letting other people take creative risk, and get the rewards for when they do that well. And, then, what we do is focus on matching the different products that are made with the right consumers, the sort of very technological aspect of matching it and streaming it. So, I would say that the scenario that you outlined would be quite a change in direction and quite unlikely. (Netflix 2011; Q4 2010 Earnings Call Transcript, January 26, 2011)

As commented upon in the previous chapter, this quote also exemplifies Hastings' rhetorical misdirection away from original programming, and emphasis upon projecting the company's *tech* identity and brand. This passage carries a note of humor when read now, given the unprecedented scale of Netflix's strategic investment of tens of billions in capital in originals over the years. This transcript even offers a notable Freudian slip, with Hastings' stumbling over and repeating a blatant falsehood regarding script-reading and creative risk decisions which the company and its executives would later admit to and even boast about engaging in in their bid for *House of Cards*. The above quote importantly comes from early 2011, marking the introduction of this question of potential original programming which we now know was a crucial turn in the story of Netflix's investor lore and brand. Even if we give Hastings some benefit of the doubt here, his "unlikely scenarios" of original production, studio investment, and creative financing have indeed come to pass, resulting in massive floods of content and capital, as streams of culture and finance have converged through the platform. This exchange of words exemplifies the *fictitious* foundation upon which the company expanded into original programming. Looking at Netflix's investor lore during this era sheds light upon its discursive misdirections, as well as the construction of the now central pillar of original programming within the company's narrative, brand identity, and strategy.

Netflix's dramatic journey began by taking a leap on one show, *House of Cards*, and now the company's current scale of production is simply unprecedented: 657 "first-run original titles" totaling 2,701 hours, or 112.5 days of original programming in 2019 alone (Prange 2020). In this final chapter, I examine how the turn to original programming emerged in 2011, and evolved into a central pillar of the company's projections of value today. In looking at this third act in the story of Netflix, I identify and interrogate the discursive strategies the company has wielded as it has evolved into a major "studio" of a new breed.

Two months after the release of Netflix's first exclusive series *Lilyhammer*, the company elaborated upon their original programming strategy in their Q1 2012 letter to Shareholders:

> One way to think of originals is in terms of brand halo. If we are able to generate critical success for our originals, it will elevate our consumer brand and drive incremental members to the service. That took HBO nearly a decade to accomplish, so we don't expect overnight results. The breadth of media coverage we already get, though, for the highly anticipated new season of "Arrested Development," as well as for "Lilyhammer" and "House of Cards," has been great. [. . .] We know we have a lot to learn in the originals area. In terms of early results, we exceeded our targets on "Lilyhammer" in terms of PR,

viewing, and critical acclaim. The show has driven millions of hours viewed, is rated highly (4 out of 5 stars on average) and generated hundreds of millions of consumer impressions with a comparatively small PR and marketing spend.

—CEO Reed Hastings & CFO David Wells (Netflix 2012 Q1 Letter to Shareholders, April 23, 8,9)

Rhetorically framing their statement as one of early confidence based upon the early reception of *Lilyhammer*'s first months of release, Hastings and Wells write at length about the value that original programming was already bringing to the company. Aimed at a skeptical financial audience still reeling from the Qwikster crash, the citation of statistics for hours watched, impressions, and ratings, as well as qualitative indicators such as their HBO self-comparison, PR, critical acclaim, and popular excitement, all served to *teach* the investing readership *how to read* this discourse of value and the new platform economics that originals would bring to Netflix.

The letter goes on:

Another way to think of originals is vertical integration; can we remove enough inefficiency from the show launch process that we can acquire content more cheaply through licensing shows directly rather than going through distributors who have already launched a show? Our on-demand and personalized platform means that we don't have to assemble a mass audience at say, 8pm on Sunday, to watch the first episode. Instead, we can give producers the opportunity to deliver us great serialized shows and we can cost-efficiently build demand over time, with members discovering these new franchises much in the same way they've discovered and come to love shows like "Mad Men" and "Breaking Bad." In this regard, we are happy to report that in terms of cost per viewing hour, which is how we evaluate content efficiency, "Lilyhammer" so far performs in line with similar premium exclusive content that we currently license.

—CEO Reed Hastings & CFO David Wells (Netflix 2012 Q1 Letter to Shareholders, April 23, 8,9)

The implication of an increasingly *inefficient* content licensing model, and by extension an increasingly competitive streaming landscape, shows how industrial convergence through vertical integration could be a potential solution to this problem. Anticipating the dwindling long-term possibilities for capitalizing on the media infrastructure of its streaming apparatus alone— subscription revenue and heightened market capitalization through pure distribution—original programming offered a way for Netflix to shift from its role as solely a distribution platform, to a content owner (or at least exclusive distribution rights owner*)*. Citing the affordances, features, and "user values" of nonlinearity, personalization, and multi-episode watching (bingeing), original programming for a *platform* is projected here as easier, more efficient, and more effective not only for users but also for producers in terms of PR and marketing spend. Importantly, this passage argues that Netflix could now *construct* and *guide* audiences to such content over time. While indicating its internal metric to measure content efficiency—cost per viewing hour—specific figures, however, were importantly withheld. As a tech company afterall, Netflix was focused upon such behavioral user data, and maintains a strong interest in keeping those numbers secret from competitors. This secrecy also conveniently allowed them to build up the *lore* of originals as valuable, successful, and efficient without necessarily having to prove it.

Expanding its project of turning film and television into content for engaging user experiences, Netflix's entrance into the original programming world took this a step further:

> As we build our capability in originals, we will have some advantages relative to our competitors. Namely, we have extensive user viewing history and ratings data to allow us to better understand potential appeal of future programs, as well as a very broad and already segmented audience. At the same time, we don't face the same pressure as linear or ad-supported online networks to deliver ratings. Finally, we should be able to use our size and international scale to bring the best original and exclusive content from anywhere in the world to anywhere in the world. This is a real advantage over our regional competitors.
>
> —CEO Reed Hastings & CFO David Wells (Netflix 2012 Q1 Letter to Shareholders, April 23, 9)

This passage is important as an admission of sorts, as it states the centrality of *data* to Netflix's programming choices, beyond licensing and recommendations to now potentially "global"[1] original content production, acquisition, and control. Here the increasingly surveillant and extractive nature of user interactions with the Netflix platform was rather framed positively as a competitive advantage to inform the production of content and the positioning of audiences alike. This quote exemplifies an important new iteration of industry lore particular to digital platforms. "Disrupting" the Nielsen household ratings system of legacy television[2]—designed to sell demographic viewing information for targeted advertising—the platform infrastructure of Netflix is *its own internal, invisible, and further privatized* Nielsen company of sorts. Rather than selling this data to industry markets, Netflix reinvests it into its decisions to license and recommend, and now personalize and produce *content.* Through its very design, Netflix turns every user into a Nielsen-esque data generator, with the *entire user base as its sample group,* rather than the hopefully representative demographic cross-section Nielsen strives for

(Pollak 2015). It is worth citing here again my definition of investor lore: "The *emergent discourses* among *investing actors* about what kinds of *user experiences* are and are not *valuable,* and *which users those experiences* will and will not *engage,*" as this model turns culture into experiences, user data into investments, and ultimately users into investors. The above quote thus exemplifies Netflix's attempt to convince investors that its platform model will be able to sustainably predict, construct, guide, and *engage user experiences* of originals as a means of *value* generation. As an evolution of Netflix's long-term brand promise of personalization, this moment, however, understated, marked a turning point within Netflix's investor lore. Here the viewing and "user engagement" data they had been collecting for sixteen years were weaponized against the owners of the very content Netflix had licensed *for* its users to engage with up until this point. Taking aim at content owners, Netflix communicated that such data now provided them with the confidence to commission original productions and exclusive rights for international distribution based upon viewing trends which suggested theoretical taste groups, audiences, and appetites for increasingly specific constellations of genres, styles, directors, writers, and stars. Where the streaming era marked an internal cannibalization of DVD-rental-by-mail, the emergence of originals signaled a slower, broader, external challenge to the media ecosystem which had sustained Netflix's licensing model. The company's lack of control over the external factors of licensing costs was thus compensated for by vertically integrating to re-organize and optimize content, data, and capital.

Evidently it would take significantly more than the emergent lore of these few paragraphs to convince investors of the potential of original programming, as the company's stock fell over fourteen points the day after the publishing of this earnings release. Wall Street remained skeptical if not frightened by this unproven spending model (Financial Content 2019). Where the 2011 announcement of the *House of Cards* deal was talked back at the time as an "experimental licensing model," Netflix's rhetoric shifted dramatically in one short year in attempt to communicate to investors the seriousness and potential of originals going forward. With their credibility and brand still bruised from the Qwikster crash, Hastings' and company realized they would have to play a longer game to claw their way back into the good graces of Wall Street.

KING CONTENT

However, after the stock hit a multiyear low of $57.85 in October 2012, Netflix would nearly triple this value by late January 2013. Jumping up by a staggering 65 points in the two days of trading after their Q4 2012 report, the company boasted an annual addition of 10 million streaming subscribers, a return to profitability, and foreshadowed the release of multiple original series. On the upswing from this ecstatic report, a GQ profile on Hastings and Sorandos titled "And the Award for the Next HBO Goes to" was also published just two days before the premiere of the first season of Netflix's flagship original *House of Cards*. The now infamous Sarandos quote "the goal is to become HBO faster than HBO can become us" came from this article, and showcased Netflix's official challenge to Hollywood's TV industry. The long-form piece features the subheading:

> The quirky little start-up that once printed money by mailing you DVDs is hell-bent on morphing into the HBO—and the network, and the any-show, any-time streaming service—of tomorrow. Can Netflix and its pathologically modest founder, Reed Hastings, pull it off? Who knows? But it's going to be fun to watch, starting this month with David Fincher's $100 million House of Cards. The only guaranteed winner in the bloody battle for the on-demand future? You. On your couch. (Hass 2013)

Fanning the flames of the rising content wars between Netflix and Hollywood, this introduction situates the user as the beneficiary of this added layer of competition in the entertainment industry—of which Netflix was now considered a part of. Emphasizing the scale and risk of Netflix's costly entrance into the content production market, this article heightened the drama of this new aspect of the company's investor lore, as well as the increasingly antagonistic—or underdog—role Netflix was now playing in Hollywood. The profile focuses primarily on Hastings but also importantly introduces Chief Content Officer Ted Sarandos, an increasingly important narrator of the company's investor lore as the company shifted into original and exclusive content strategies. Sketching portraits of these characters/narrators through personal stories and detailed anecdotes, the author Nancy Hass provided ample room for these figureheads of the brand to showcase their disruptive philosophy. She writes of Sarandos:

> [His] seductive pitch to today's new breed of TV auteurs: a huge audience, real money, no meddlesome executives ("I'm not going to give David Fincher notes"), no pilots (television's great sucking hole of money and hope), and a full-season commitment. (Hass 2013)

"Innovating" traditional approaches to the production, distribution, and audiencing of "quality" televisual content, the anticipation of both Hollywood and Wall Street was growing to see how the experiment of *House of Cards*, and the new platform model it represented, would play out. The quote above exemplifies the emerging motif of "creative freedom" in regard to original programming that Netflix sought to foreground in its investor lore. While stated briefly here, this line is indicative of Netflix's communicative strategy to attract top creative talent for their originals, and thus convince investors that they could continue to do so. Since the inception of originals, Netflix has had actors and directors champion this idea about how "liberating" their creative experiences were with the company, as they were not beholden to pilots, weekly releases, advertisers, smaller budgets, and the administration of each of these factors. Indeed a critical, yet neglected, aspect of the creative labor performed by such actors and showrunners is to be brand ambassadors and paratextual narrators of investor lore off screen, of which I discuss later in this chapter.

The conclusion of Hass' article takes the reader to the wrap party of the resuscitated fourth season of *Arrested Development*, now a Netflix Original. Hass frames an awkward interaction between Hastings and Fox's head of digital distribution Peter Levinsohn. Beneath a veneer of civility, the star tech CEO seems to gloat over the linear TV executive, relishing in the joy of his own clever disruption while feigning a spirit of industrial collegiality and collaboration. Positioning Netflix as an emerging threat to linear television and its traditional modes of production, this article thematizes the new competition between streaming and linear TV as a race to internet TV dominance; a race in which Netflix had a considerable head start. Articles such as this one furthered Netflix's teleological lore of the *inevitable online future* of television; as Sarandos' pithy HBO remark made clear: the race to dominate both "quality" original content *and* online distribution markets were now one in the same. In other words media convergence 101: content, communications, and computing industries increasingly overlapping due to the shared reliances and efficiencies of digitization and now platformization. Invoking the imagery of a race in which Netflix had a technological head start, this article contributed to Netflix's lore of convergence and disruption, bolstering the old adage that "fortune"—meaning both luck *and* wealth in this case—"favours the bold."

> Dear Fellow Shareholders, In Q1, we added over 3 million streaming members, bringing us to more than 36 million, who collectively enjoyed on Netflix over 4 billion hours of films and TV shows.
>
> —CEO Reed Hastings & CFO David Wells (Netflix 2013, Q1 Letter to Shareholders, April 22, 1)

Rhetorically emphasizing the scale of the company's growth and success,— *and importantly their built-in ability to accurately measure such growth metrics*—these opening lines of the Q1 2013 investor letter boast the simultaneous quarterly growth of subscriptions (revenue) and the unprecedented growth of their streaming consumption (time, attention, and user-audience data). Underneath this leading message, a spreadsheet (table 3.1) showcases the performance of Q1 2013 compared to the previous four quarters, divided into the categories of domestic streaming, international streaming, domestic DVD, and total global figures. The visualization of data displayed here speaks to the shifting priorities of Netflix, guiding the reader to interpolate seasonal and annual trends and temporalities in membership (growth in streaming, decline in DVD), revenue, operating income, profit margins, and earnings per share.

After outlining improvements and efficiencies in both domestic and international streaming markets, the letter shifts to examine the new strategy of

Table 3.1   Netflix Q1 2013 Earnings Data (Netflix 2013)

(in millions except per share data)	Q1 '12	Q2 '12	Q3 '12	Q4 '12	Q1 '13
Domestic Streaming:					
Net Additions	1.74	0.53	1.16	2.05	2.03
Total Members	23.41	23.94	25.10	27.15	29.17
Paid Members	22.02	22.69	23.80	25.47	27.91
Revenue ($)	507	533	556	589	639
Contribution Profit* ($)	72	87	96	113	131
Contribution Margin* (%)	14.3	16.4	17.2	19.2	20.6
International Streaming:					
Net Additions	1.21	0.56	0.69	1.81	1.02
Total Members	3.07	3.62	4.31	6.12	7.14
Paid Members	2.41	3.02	3.69	4.89	6.33
Revenue ($)	43	65	78	101	142
Contribution Profit* ($)	103	89	92	105	77
Contribution Margin*					
Domestic DVD:					
Total Members	10.09	9.24	8.61	8.22	7.98
Revenue ($)	320	291	271	254	243
Contribution Profit ($)	146	134	131	128	113
Global:					
Revenue	870	889	905	945	1,024
Operating Income (Loss) ($)	(2)	16	16	20	32
Net Income (Loss)** ($)	(5)	6	8	8	3
Net Income Excluding Debt Extinguishment Loss ($)	—	—	—	—	19
EPS** ($)	(0.08)	0.11	0.13	0.13	0.05
EPS Excluding Debt Extinguishment Loss ($)	—	—	—	—	0.31
Free Cash Flow ($)	2	11	(20)	(51)	(42)
Shares (FD)	55.5	58.8	58.7	59.1	60.1

*Contribution profit and margin for prior periods reflect reclassification of marketing overhead costs to G&A.
**Net Income/EPS includes a $25M loss on extinguishment of debt ($16M net of tax).

"Original Series," now its very own section in the quarterly letter to shareholders since Q1 2012.

> On February 1, we premiered all 13 episodes of House of Cards to enormous popular and critical acclaim. The global viewing and high level of engagement with the show increased our confidence in our ability to pick shows Netflix members will embrace and to pick partners skilled at delivering a great series. The high level of viewer satisfaction implies we are able to target the right audience without the benefit of existing broadcast or cable viewing data and the strong viewing across all our markets gives us faith in our ability to create global content brands in a cost-effective, efficient way.
>
> —CEO Reed Hastings & CFO David Wells (Netflix 2013; Q1 Letter to Shareholders, April 22, 4)

Global, engagement, confidence, satisfaction, targeting, data, efficiency. This introduction to the original programming section emphasizes the power of the Netflix platform model to efficiently *pick* content and content providers to match with *target* audiences and publish such content in the most *engaging* way. As a recent Harvard Business Review article highlights, internet economies of scale create efficiencies and synergies (network effects) not only in strict financial terms, but now importantly in terms of the "richness" or utility of data to understand, predict, and guide user behavior and thus satisfaction, brand strength, user growth, and so on:

> In the internet economy, firms that achieve higher "volume" than competitors (that is, attract more platform participants) offer a higher average value per transaction. That's because the larger the network, the better the matches between supply and demand and the richer the data that can be used to find matches. Greater scale generates more value, which attracts more participants, which creates more value—another virtuous feedback loop that produces monopolies. (Van Alstyne, Parker, and Choudary 2016, 58)

The former quarterly report quote mirrors the latter quite closely, and 2013's *House of Cards* was a crucial moment in mythologizing the potential power of this platform model and the valuable new media economics of network effects. With the company's flagship global content brand campaign for *House of Cards* successfully becoming an undeniable cultural *and industrial* phenomenon, Netflix was able to leverage such sociocultural saliency as an indication of the brand power of the show, and by extension the company. Notably any *quantitative* metrics surrounding the show's success were strategically withheld, clearly communicating that such viewer data would remain proprietary. When asked specifically about measuring and communicating

House of Cards as a successful investment in the Q1 2013 earnings call, Hastings' encouraged investors rather to see the forest for the trees, to have faith in what this model does for the company overall, as opposed to focusing on any individual title. *You* invest in Netflix, not just *House of Cards*. Here *House of Cards* proved to be symbolic of an emergent storyline within the company's lore which sought to inspire belief from investors that original production could offer an alternative, supplementary content model as opposed to licensing alone. Attributing the quarterly jump in subscribers largely to the release of *House of Cards*, Wall Street was evidently, if not temporarily, convinced of the potential of this new model, with Netflix's stock value rising 53 points (over 30 percent at that time) in two days after the publication of the Q1 2013 report. The investor lore for original programming was working, generating fictitious capital through capitalizing on fiction.

Overall, momentum would continue to build for the lore of Netflix's original content model, sparking a multiyear upward trajectory for the company's valuation. Dips in the company's stock price became predictable if subscriber growth numbers were lower than expected, and unpredictable general dips in global financial markets also affected the stock temporarily but overall it was again onward and upward. Netflix's new investor lore, strengthened by Originals, was working. In other words, Netflix's lore of streaming distribution, original content production, and international expansion attracted increasing volumes of financial capital, as the company captured more and more users with this model. With successful Original brands such as *House of Cards*, *Orange Is the New Black*, *Hemlock Grove*, *Bojack Horseman*, and *Arrested Development*, the first "slate" of original programming in these first few years comprised a tiny but meaningful portion of the Netflix catalogue, communicating to investors the company's ability to create and sustain popular content brands, and claiming that this helps attract users. Without releasing viewer data, investors and researchers (such as myself), have no way of verifying this claim, making its rhetorical framing and *narrative* perpetuation all the more important to analyze. Regardless of its validity, the value and success of this promissory lore of consistently providing engaging user experiences through originals remains integral to the overall Netflix brand (and) narrative.

In a show of confidence the company issued a 7-for-1 stock split, from just over $700 per share to $100 in July of 2015, increasing the liquidity, flexibility, and accessibility of their stock for purchase and trade. The inflation of the stock to such heights evidences the successful lore and "comeback" story of the company's financial communications and branding since 2011. Beyond the scaling of their digital provision of video entertainment, it was also the discursive assemblage of language, statistics, and economics which sold this financial narrative of "future value" to investors. This faith from Wall Street importantly reinforced Netflix's industrial strategies, operations, and of course the lore which communicates such practices as valuable. The positive feedback circuit of discourse and value here betrays the self-fulfilling prophecy of successful investor lore; if enough investors *believe,* the effects of their mutual faith and investment drive value. Like the time, attention, sociality, and capital that users invest in Netflix and its content brands (generating behavioral data, revenue, word-of-mouth buzz, and free marketing for the company), the time, attention, sociality, and capital that *investors* dedicate to Netflix's stock and story produces similar effects for a financial audience (perhaps desperately) looking for a valuable story. As this monograph has hopefully demonstrated, the biggest, most influential Netflix Original has really been the multisited project of its investor lore, pushing around hundreds of billions of dollars, data points, hours, words, and images.

By the end of 2015 the company would boast nearly 75 million subscribers in sixty different countries, with international user additions outpacing domestic growth by a factor of five (Netflix 2015). Originals represented Netflix's ability to adapt to an increasingly expensive content licensing landscape, and also strategically circumvented many of the political and geographic strictures of IP law (Lobato 2017, 2019). If Netflix was the exclusive distributor if not producer of a content title, it could easily give itself global rights in perpetuity to such content, increasing the spatiotemporal reach of and *returns on* such investments.

TALKING ABOUT A "GLOBAL" REVOLUTION

In early January of 2016 Hastings delivered a keynote presentation at the Consumer Electronics Showcase, the massive international tech industry trade show held in Las Vegas annually. Joined by Sarandos, a host of actors, and a slew of Netflix Original previews, Hastings used this global stage to boast of his company's successes, and offer a vision of the future: a global TV network. Indicative of the fantastical ethos of Silicon Valley's "disruptive innovation" narrative, this presentation told the story of how Netflix rose to be the best in the industry, and promised to always innovate its way into the future to maintain such self-appointed dominance. The object of Netflix's "innovative" desire, and thus potential future, expressed at CES 2016 was *global storytelling*; a convergent narrative of technology and entertainment from which a "global internet TV network" providing *Netflix Global Originals* would emerge.

This industry trade show is one of the richest displays of this "third season" of Netflix and its investor lore; amplifying the company's messaging of how their technological innovations have led to the "best user experience of TV." Alongside the company's foundational discourses of user convenience, choice, and ease, the emerging themes of this event focused upon the quality, creative freedom, and "globality" of Netflix and its originals. To lead up to these new themes, Hastings offered a brief revisionist history of entertainment technologies:

> Entertainment and technology are continuing to transform each other as they have been doing for over a hundred years. From radio to broadcast TV, broadcast TV to cable TV and now to internet TV with each of these bringing a better experience. With broadcast TV starting in the 1950s you could watch video in your home and that was a miracle at the time but with broadcast TV you had only a few networks and so not much choice. Then came cable TV where you had hundreds of networks to scroll through but what consumers really wanted was to be able to choose when to watch. The VCR let them do that to some degree, recording films and TV series to watch later. The DVR made the VCR a little less clunky. The VCR and DVR were early efforts to give people what they wanted: on-demand television. With the Internet, we can finally give people what they have always wanted, we can now put consumers across the world in the driver's seat when it comes to when and where they want to watch. Internet TV allows us to redefine what is possible. Great stories at your fingertips on your Smart TV, on your phone, tablet, and laptop. You can start, pause, and resume watching whenever and wherever you feel like it. You don't have to sit through commercials or be at the mercy of an 8pm tune in, you just click and watch. A simple revolutionary shift from corporate to consumer control. The Netflix service is personalized for you and every other member of your household. We offer movies and TV shows for every taste and every age. Shows that inform, that provoke, that engage, that delight. We are just beginning to break down the barriers so the world's best storytellers can reach audiences all over the world.
>
> —CEO Reed Hastings (Netflix CES 2016 Keynote)

Narrating a specific and convergent history of home entertainment, Hastings' rhetorically positions the wants and needs of the consumer throughout the twentieth and twenty-first centuries. Unsurprisingly, through this discursive narrative of "innovation and progress," the Netflix CEO elucidates how linear TV's frustrating lack of choice and scheduled programming have been defeated by the convergence of TV, consumer electronics, and the internet: *streaming*. Hastings' remarks reflect a new politicization of time in late capitalism, as the leisure activity of watching television now must be as flexible and on-demand as contemporary organizations of labor. You can watch "whatever" you want, "wherever" you might be, with the technological infrastructures you have invested in (broadband connections, data plans, screen devices), "whenever" (or if ever) you have the time for leisure. Moreover this discourse of consumer choice, coded with ideas of economic and cultural accessibility to entertainment, also indicate the internet's great illusion of freedom, which overwhelms the user with increasing volumes of information and choice to ultimately guide and surveille user navigation, consumption, and behavior into more predictable and thus potentially profitable "experiences." The supposed mitigation of this option paralysis is evident in the user interface and user experience design, with algorithmically informed "recommended for you," "because you watched" and "trending now" category banners, as well as hundreds of micro-genre tags[3] and lists to *channel* user consumption. All of this works to fulfill the performative promise of Netflix's investor lore to personalize—*guide*—user behavior.

One needn't look further than the autoplay function after the completion of a series episode to understand how Netflix's user interface and user experience design encourages and channels such behaviors and patterns of consumption. Such design seeks to generate ever more user data and viewership, which can in turn be celebrated, albeit opaquely, as successful and efficient content to investors: a promise fulfilled. The strategic shift in focus from film to TV content during the transition to streaming and the rollout of original programming further indicates Netflix's simultaneous production of audiences *and* content, as an industrial "synergy" and optimization of capital and investment: cost per viewing hour.

By declaring linear television's problems of choice and scheduling to be solved by streaming, this keynote argued that *space* was the final frontier or challenge which could also be "disrupted," flattened, and thus eventually capitalized upon.

> We're shooting a sports comedy in Mexico, a crime drama in Italy, a dystopian film about bioengineering in Korea. The possibilities of building connections between cultures and people are endless and important, that's why we're here to talk this morning. We're gonna talk about how the Internet is changing television and how we're at the start of a global revolution.
>
> —CEO Reed Hastings (Netflix CES 2016 Keynote)

The rollout of Netflix's international expansion had been slow and steady in the five years leading up to this event, with the company taking initial losses as investments to "break in" to new markets. The quote above showcases the emergence of Netflix's discourse of "glocalization": producing local, non-English content to distribute globally and instantaneously. Beyond just operating and licensing *some* local language content for that region or territory, CES 2016 was a major platform for Netflix to disseminate its message of international original production, and the "endless possibilities" that this "global revolution of internet TV" could provide.

Netflix's construction of "globality" is eerily reminiscent of nineteenth-century German thinker Johann Wolfgang Goethe and compares his philosophy of world literature for some insightful similarities.[4] In 1827, Goethe wrote in a letter to his friend, the poet Johann Eckermann:

> I am more and more convinced, [. . .] that poetry is the universal possession of mankind, revealing itself everywhere, and at all times, in hundreds and hundreds of men. [. . .] I therefore like to look about me in foreign nations, and advise everyone to do the same. National literature is now rather an unmeaning term; the epoch of World literature is at hand, and every one must strive to hasten its approach. But, while we thus value what is foreign, we must not bind ourselves to anything in particular, and regard it as a model. We must not give this value to the Chinese, or the Servian, or Calderon, or the Nibelungen; but if we really want a pattern, we must always return to the ancient Greeks, in whose works the beauty of mankind is constantly represented. All the rest we must look at only historically, appropriating to ourselves what is good, so far as it goes.
>
> —Goethe, 1827 (2011, 322; trans. Oxenford)

The parallels between Hastings' remark of a "global [TV] revolution" and Goethe's Euro-philic musings upon the idea of a "world literature" are many-fold. Like Goethe's perhaps well-intentioned, but ultimately white bourgeois gesture to translate as many literary works into as many languages as possible, Hastings' global television network proclaims a similarly utopian vision of transnational cultural exchange, albeit conveniently aligned with potential flows of global capital. I include the last two lines of Goethe's quote, as its citation generally tends to get cut off before his addendum defending and championing the Western canon. Where Goethe sought to appropriate world literature for the cultural value and human insight it might offer to the "enlightened West," Hastings' sings a similar tune regarding the potential financial value and behavioral data "World TV" might offer to Wall Street, Silicon Valley, and the largely Western loci of financial, technological, and cultural power. The parallels to modernist, enlightenment thinking should call attention to the character of our new age of techno-financial rationality.[5]

In an attempt to further project an ethos of global sharing and storytelling, CCO Ted Sarandos took the stage to explain the philosophy, value, and potential scale of Netflix's global original programming strategy.[6]

> At Netflix we have what we call the freedom and responsibility culture, which means that Netflix executives get a lot of freedom to innovate in our fast-moving

business. It also means that we're responsible for delivering the goods; we treat the filmmakers the exact same way. We hire strong creatives. We let them create compelling worlds [. . .] It is true that we believe in quality: great visuals, well-written scripts, awards worthy acting, but as you saw in that first sizzle reel, we love stories of all sorts: highbrow, lowbrow, funny, sad, scary, you name it. We have that luxury thanks to the internet. Linear TV—the kind we all grew up on—must aggregate a large audience at a given time of day and hope that whatever they're showing will attract enough viewers. With Netflix, members could enjoy a show anytime, and based on their viewing habits we could put the right one in front of them each and every time. That means we can spend less on marketing and still generate higher viewership even from smaller quirkier less traditionally commercial material.

—CCO Ted Sarandos (Netflix CES 2016 Keynote)

Referencing Netflix's infamous corporate culture[7]—which prioritizes employee performance over rules and regulations—Sarandos argues that the same philosophy they apply to computer engineering and executive performance should also apply to the creative work of cultural production. Putting forth the idea that this "culture of freedom" will allow for more compelling, diverse, quality content, Sarandos explains how their platform model of distribution (and promotion) encourages and optimizes capital invested in originals. Citing also the promise of personalization, Sarandos communicates how the affordance and power of recommendation algorithms increases and streamlines engagement with content, thus saving on external marketing costs. He goes on to further elaborate upon how Netflix's platform-studio model identifies, guides, and produces audiences for such content:

Now at Netflix we famously use big data to help us size our investments in different types of programming. This allows us to deliver a spectacularly broad range of series and films to our members without having to worry about the reach of any one single title at any one moment. We can have content that appeals to a five-year-old, a teen, or their grandparents all living in the same household. Because of this unique strength we can commit to producing and publishing books rather than chapters. We can give creators the chance to concentrate on multi-episode story arcs rather than pilots. A creator can work on episode 11, confident that very recently the viewer has enjoyed episode 1 through 10. They could develop episodes that are not all exactly 22 or 44 minutes long they could take 10 episodes or 20 episodes to tell their stories. Pilots, the fall season, summer repeats, live ratings, all of the constraints of linear television are falling away one by one.

—CCO Ted Sarandos (Netflix CES 2016 Keynote)

This quote clearly evidences Lotz' theorization that the affordance of nonlinear programming increases the efficiencies or "synergies" of a vertically integrated model of content provision: production, programming, promotion, recommendation, and distribution through scaled consumption.[8] Sarandos and Hastings both cite the emergent phenomenon of "binging" in this keynote, arguing that it adds user value, and frees creative talent to "innovate" the art of storytelling with less structure—which of course they argue further makes for better, "more meaningful" user experiences.[9] As "binging" entered the popular vernacular, its association with Netflix offered an invaluable form of brand recognition, and is indeed a popular, multi-sited component of Netflix's investor lore. Claiming to disrupt linear TV and its constraints to an audience of tech investors, Sarandos appealed to the industry's appetite for such a narrative of innovation and an innovation of narrative itself.

After explaining and projecting Netflix's original programming lore, Sarandos invited the stars of four Netflix Originals up on stage to do the same: Chelsea Handler of docu-series *Chelsea Does*, Will Arnett of *Arrested Development*, *Bojack Horseman*, and *Flaked*, Krysten Ritter of Marvel's *Jessica Jones*, and Wagner Moura of *Narcos*. Emphasizing the "global" reach of Netflix Originals, the guests shared their experiences of traveling the world, promoting their titles, and working with Netflix. Like prior endorsements from David Fincher and Kevin Spacey, these stars also became both narrators *of*, and figures *within* Netflix's lore of global original programming.[10] The emergent discourse here was of Netflix as a home for creative talent and "innovative" storytelling with a "global audience." Thus the conversation between these actors and performers rhetorically thematized the creative freedom of working for Netflix, alongside the joys of instantaneous international distribution. As a comedian and experienced talk-show host, Handler took on the role of moderator, leading the discussion among this panel of actors ever toward topics of international accessibility to content and the experience of working with Netflix as a creator.

Quotes from each of the panel members further evidence these emergent themes within Netflix's investor lore:

> One of the things that makes me really happy about Narcos is that American audiences embraced a show that's I think 70%? [. . .] spoken in Spanish [. . .] It's pretty cool!
>
> —Wagner Moura (Netflix CES 2016 Keynote)

> We went to Italy, Spain, Japan, Brazil [. . .] It's been completely mind-blowing to go and promote your show in all of these different countries. Jessica Jones is a

really unique character that we haven't seen before. The superhero genre is kind of a boys playground, so it's really exciting to have this amazing, you know, female character with a global audience come out, you know, making some noise. It's been incredibly exciting. [. . .] When I was watching the show at the end there's all of these different pages crediting the actors that do the dubbing so that goes on for pages and pages [. . .] In so many countries—yeah—it's crazy.

—Krysten Ritter (Netflix CES 2016 Keynote)

When I started working with Netflix was on Arrested Development and that was sort of three four years ago, and it was Ted and Reed and some dude, you know, who was like doing accounting on the back of a napkin. The company has grown and the audience has grown and I gotta say this, it's interesting from then to now, you know, doing Bojack and watching, you know, the global impact. You know I went with Kristin for part of that trip we were in Spain and Italy and having people . . . knowing that they're watching the show day in day at the same time that we are here which is such a different. . .as Ted said before we're just throwing out the old paradigm is completely gone and now everything that you do is immediately available, you know, and all these countries around the world it's pretty amazing.

—Will Arnett (Netflix CES 2016 Keynote)

It's such a nice place to work when you can kind of go and create a vision and then you guys are progressive enough to say go do it and then all of a sudden that's done. I pitched you four documentaries, you said yeah they sound like great ideas and that was it and I was like—I mean that's probably not a great way to tell Reed that you're running things—it's a great place to work and that's all I have to say on the topic.

—Chelsea Handler (Netflix CES 2016 Keynote)

With some tactful banter, Handler's guidance of the discussion sought to showcase Netflix as a progressive yet edgy new player in the entertainment industry; a new, tech approach to TV. Each of these above quotes elucidates this message. For example, Moura (a Brazilian actor) learned Spanish to play the role of Pablo Escobar, and speaks to the authenticity of *Narcos'* predominantly Spanish dialogue. Contrasting themselves from the supposedly conventional industry lore that subtitled content would not reach or engage popular audiences, Moura and Sarandos provide anecdotal evidence on the contrary, and speak of the show's wide viewership in America and beyond, without of course sharing specifics. Furthering this point, Ritter and later Arnett also cite how "exciting" and "amazing" it is to witness the "global" reach of their work, made possible by Netflix's investment in expanding its international streaming infrastructure, dubbing, and subtitling. In relation to Netflix's reputation as a home for progressive content, both Ritter and Handler also importantly frame the company as a supporter and champion female-led content, from the super hero action genre, to Handler's unconventional and wide-reaching docu-series, of which Handler boasts "they paid me to do drugs! I went to Peru and did Ayahuasca. . . . It's the best job in the world everybody!"

Arnett's account also highlights how much Netflix—and its global audiences—have grown since he began working with the company on the revamp of *Arrested Development* in 2013. Handler's final quote concluded this somewhat awkward but nonetheless insightful discussion of Netflix's identity as a growing producer of content, and the new paradigm defining the company's strategy. This move to enlist creative talent to be first-person narrators of Netflix's investor lore for original programming sought to increase the company's credibility as not only a studio, but an innovator and disruptor to traditional studio practices: open to new types, formats, and approaches to creating and providing content.

Endorsements from such actors here also extended Netflix's challenge to Hollywood, in bidding not only for the time and attention of user-audiences but also creative talent. The central message thematized here was that Netflix is a better home for creators, as their content could push traditional boundaries in terms of genre, form, and representation, and would also have an instantaneous global release and thus potential audience. The argument put forth here was that if Netflix could attract top talent, it could provide quality content, maintaining and luring in ever more users, revenue, and data to inform which talent the company might pursue and so on; yet another feedback loop of value.

The climactic finale of this event featured a bold announcement from Hastings; a grand reveal contradicting the timeline laid out in his own introduction by Consumer Technology Association president and CEO Gary Shapiro.

> We're fortunate that he's agreed to share time with us to talk about building a global internet TV network as Netflix intends to be in nearly every country by the end of 2016. Ladies and gentlemen please join me in welcoming the chief executive officer and co-founder of Network—Netflix and our keynote speaker this morning Reed Hastings.
>
> —Gary Shapiro (Netflix CES 2016 Keynote).

While we have been here on stage at CES we switched Netflix on in Azerbaijan, in Vietnam, in India, in Nigeria, in Poland, in Russia, in Saudi Arabia, in

Singapore, in South Korea, in Turkey, in Indonesia, and in a hundred and thirty new countries. While you have been listening to me talk, the Netflix service has gone live in nearly every country of the world, except China, where we hope to also be in the future. Today, right now, you are witnessing the birth of a global TV network—and I do mean the birth. Today we are offering consumers around the world our incredible global catalog of original content available around the world including licensed feature films and series. We've also added Korean and Arabic and Chinese, to bring our supported languages to 21. From today onwards we listen, we learn, we improve, we add more languages, more content, more ways for people to engage with Netflix over the next several years. Our goal is to offer an ever improving service with incredible Netflix shows and films coming from storytellers around the world to people around the world. The global potential is both a joy and a challenge to fulfill. Whether you were in Sydney or St. Petersburg, Singapore or Seoul, Santiago or Saskatoon, you now can be part of the Internet TV revolution. No more waiting, no more watching on a schedule that's not your own. No more frustration, just Netflix, how, when, and wherever you are in the world. Today you have witnessed an incredible event. Thank you all for coming.

—CEO Reed Hastings (Netflix CES 2016 Keynote)

Projecting an image of a worldwide streaming service, Hastings' conclusion at CES 2016 claimed in many ways to conquer the sociopolitical and cultural complexities of space itself; the divisions of borders and language, the uneven global infrastructures of capital and power. Aligned with Netflix's brand association of instantaneity, Hastings' announcement of the "global switch-on"—like the publishing of a Netflix Original title itself—functioned as a metanarrative for Netflix's transnational ambitions, and the value this now represents in its investor lore. The narrative "twist" or reveal of Netflix being apparently a full year ahead of schedule for its global expansion turned what would have been a rollout into a launch: "no more waiting" for this so-called "global" Internet TV revolution. However, while the "globality" of Netflix's international network is wildly uneven, inaccessible, and well contested, the rhetoric of this event solidified the aspirations of the company to rapidly expand in the face of an increasingly competitive domestic streaming industry. Beyond Hulu and Amazon, a range of major tech and entertainment giants such as Apple, Google/YouTube, Disney, HBO, Facebook, Comcast, and AT&T, among a host of other smaller companies would all announce plans to enter into the SVOD space in some capacity around this time (if they hadn't already). The flipside of the success of Netflix's investor lore—evident in its rapidly rising stock value, revenue, and user base—was also a rising wave of domestic competition. From here international expansion thus offered a way for

Netflix to differentiate itself, with a wide range of alternative markets to enter, where anyone with an internet-connected screen could theoretically become a potential user. These broader industrial shifts signal how the narrative of value that streaming represented has become increasingly accepted by all stakeholders: users, investors, executives, creators, coders, and most importantly other tech and culture industry competitors. In America, the home of many of these converging tech and media giants, the rise of Netflix alongside major shifts in internet infrastructures and consumer technologies (and behaviors) produced the conditions for such acceptance of the narrative of streaming video as an inevitable, ubiquitous, *valuable* future. As this moment arrived, global originals and the infrastructure of a global delivery network thus represented Netflix's newest innovation and a head start in the streaming wars to come.

SCALE, RISK, RHETORIC, REWARD?

The content just keeps improving, and that keeps the word-of-mouth growing. So we're very excited about that formula.

—CEO Reed Hastings (Netflix Earnings Call Q1 2016, April 18)

Following CES, the Q1 2016 earnings report showed a relatively modest, yet still record-breaking increase in total subscribers, bringing the global total to over 81 million. The report led with the excitement of the CES global expansion announcement and attributed the growth in user acquisitions to this, as well as the release of a slate of original programs: *Making A Murderer* (a late December debut), *Fuller House* (February), *House of Cards* Season 4 (March) and *Daredevil* Season 2 (March). The range of content cited here is telling: a true crime docu-series, a remake of a popular 1990s family drama, the continuation of their flagship prestige drama, and the renewal of one of many superhero action series. Netflix was continuing to provide content for a wide range of audiences, with an increasing percentage of Originals in their catalogue, and in popular culture more generally.

The report addressed the international market challenges of language accessibility and few digital payment options, but nonetheless argued that the release of a wave of local language content under production in Mexico, Brazil, Columbia, Italy, France, Germany, and Japan in the coming quarters would be central to sustaining the company's international growth. The location of these non-English-language Originals indicate further which markets Netflix was primarily focused on developing, and what types or brands of content could produce and sustain audiences, be they local or worldwide.

Interpolating patterns from the data within and across markets with high rates of internet penetration, Netflix hoped to identify audiences and taste communities by genre, style, form, and star power in these new potential markets.

Take, for example, Adam Sandler's four-film deal with Netflix, each of which was panned by American critics and audiences alike, but were immensely popular internationally, specifically in Latin America (Garcia 2015). While perhaps idiosyncratic, this example elucidates the potential transnational flows of data, content, and capital enabled by the platform model, justified and organized by its investor lore. By producing any original—English-language or "global"—and marketing and distributing this content through strategically guided, algorithmically informed UI and UX design, the potential to achieve global economies of scale was also clearly heightened by Netflix's international launch. What failed in the domestic box office markets of yesterday could now potentially succeed on the small screens of the world.

When asked about the increasingly large budgets of Netflix's major (TV) titles: *House of Cards, Stranger Things, The Crown,* and *The Get Down,* Netflix's chief narrators expressed yet again their unflinching faith in, and endorsement of *scaled investment:*

> You should think about it that those big productions play much more like big blockbuster films. And the fact that not only do they get more watching in the US, but they travel much better too. So you see in all these non-English speaking territories, these series performed very well.
>
> —CCO Ted Sarandos (Netflix 2016a, Q1 Earnings Call, April 18)

> It suggests an increase in return on spending if anything. That is, when you spend on the big items they go much, much further than a whole lot of substitutable content. So we're interested in both spectacular content and spectacular membership growth.
>
> —CEO Reed Hastings (Netflix 2016a, Q1 Earnings Call, April 18)

Boasting of the unprecedented scale of Netflix's content budgeting, both Sarandos and Hastings' double-down here on the media economics of this choice, appealing, as always, to the *faith* of the investor in lieu of sharing any financial metrics or viewer data to support such confidence. The coming quarters and years would expand upon this rhetorical and industrial strategy, championing increasingly high production and licensing costs as the main way to ever improve the Netflix user experience, and thus drive subscriber growth worldwide.

We are incredibly excited about all the projects we have underway for our global members, no matter their age, taste or cultural background; in 2017, we plan to invest over $6 billion on content on a P&L basis (up from $5 billion in 2016).

—CEO Reed Hastings & CFO David Wells (Netflix 2017, Q4 2016 Earnings Report)

The rhetorical weight behind an additional *billion* dollars of spending projected both boldness and confidence with respect to Netflix's emerging production and licensing model in the mid-2010s. Despite brief seasonal declines, the overall upward trend of user growth backed this aggressive strategy, funded largely through re-investing revenue, debt financing, and obligatory long term payments, the scale of which can be seen in table 3.2. As the company approached nearly 100 million subscribers, questions began to arise as to just how big could Netflix grow: just how scalable and valuable could Netflix's future be? And who or what might stand in the way of maintaining such growth and sustaining the fantastical narrative of Netflix's investor lore?

MOVE FAST AND BREAK BEATS

A notable example of failure, here also a failed performative, is the Netflix Original series *The Get Down*. Directed by the acclaimed Baz Luhrmann, and

Table 3.2   Netflix's Increasing Scale of Investment and Debt-Funding since Its Inception in 1997 (Crunchbase 2020)

Announced Date	Transaction Name	Number of Investors	Money Raised	Lead Investors
April 24, 2018	Post-IPO Debt	—	$1.9B	—
February 4, 2014	Post-IPO Debt	—	$400M	—
January 29, 2013	Post-IPO Debt	—	$500M	—
November 21, 2011	Post-IPO Debt	1	$200M	TCV
April 17, 2000	Series E Funding	3	$50M	—
July 7, 1999	Series D Funding	3	$30.3M	Groupe Arnault
February 1, 1999	Series C Funding	4	$15.2M	—
June 1, 1998	Series B Funding	2	$6M	Institution Venture Partners (IVP)
March 1, 1998	Series A Funding	—	$250K	—
October 1, 1997	Series A Funding	2	$2M	Reed Hastings

set in 1970s New York at the twilight of disco and dawn of hip-hop, the first and only season of this musical drama was estimated to cost roughly $120 million. With the profile of this auteur and high production value, *The Get Down* was the first Netflix show of such size to be canceled after just one season, opening up a conversation about the sustainability and efficacy of Netflix's original programming strategy. With other Netflix titles *Marco Polo* and *Sense8* also contemporaneously canceled, the executives were understandably questioned on this point in interviews at this time.

> Failure is not such a bad thing, and if you're not failing, you—maybe you're not trying hard enough. [. . .] We have a good hit rate, and even with the recent cancellations [. . .] 93% of our shows have been renewed. So you make—you want to be introspective and look at that and say, "Are we being adventurous enough?"
>
> —CCO Ted Sarandos (Netflix 2017, Q2 Earnings Call, July 17)

> You should have more things that don't work out, you have to get more aggressive. [. . .] The drive toward conformity as you grow is more substantial. As a leader, you want to drive people to take more risks (Hastings, as quoted in Wallenstein 2017).

These responses evince the bold, if not pathological, optimism of Silicon Valley, framing the scale of failure as relative to the willingness of the company to take risks: "move fast and break things."[11] As Sarandos clearly stated, these cancellations were predominantly the exceptions to the majority of successes represented by Netflix's original content strategy. However, the rate of Netflix's cancellations has gone up in recent years alongside their scaled increase in original production. In its Q4 2017 letter to shareholders, Netflix further stated, "Our goal is to work directly with the best talent to bring amazing stories to our members all over the world," announcing vague "overall deals" with the creators of *Stranger Things* (Shawn Levy), and *Orange Is the New Black* and *GLOW* (Jenji Kohan). Again, reminiscent of the studio system of early to mid-twentieth-century Hollywood, Netflix's lore of not only attracting but maintaining relationships with top talent was again cited here. By the end of 2017, the company's executives boasted of their international profitability for the first time and announced a plan to further scale global programming accordingly with thirty international originals from France, India, Korea, Poland, and Japan (Netflix 2018, Q4 2017 Letter to Shareholders).

Since the *House of Cards* announcement of "partnership" with David Fincher 2011, Netflix has now penned TV and film deals alike with an increasingly long list of notable, acclaimed auteurs: The Coen Brothers, Guillermo Del Toro, Alfonso Cuaron, Martin Scorsese, Bong Joon-ho, Steven

Soderberg, and Qaushiq Mukherjee, rhetorically mobilizing the prestige of these directors to legitimize the platform's ability to attract "top talent." Other content deals such as the eight-show deal with Shonda Rhimes' Shondaland production company, the acquisition of popular comic book "IP universe" Millarworld, and a multiyear deal with the Obamas, provocatively highlight the scale, creativity, and notoriety of Netflix's content partnerships to add anticipatory value: *what will content from the Obamas look like?* With the lore of the Global Original established, such announcements are a new constant, with the company frequently repeating and citing the successes of their content model in efforts to bring into being and maintain its lore of talent attraction and value generation. The steadily increasing volume of company press releases further evidences the scaled expansion of Netflix's investor lore and communications. According to the Netflix Press Release Archive, the company has gone from publishing just over two releases per month in 2015, to over a post a day in 2019 on average. These official releases, alongside seemingly endless articles on Netflix in popular and trade presses—for tech, entertainment, *and* finance publications—all contribute to the buzz around Netflix, negotiating or further entrenching the company's investor lore.

THE ART OF THE FORECAST: CLOUDY
FOR THE FORESEEABLE FUTURE(S)

Our quarterly guidance is our internal forecast at the time we report and we strive for accuracy. In Q2, we underestimated the popularity of our strong slate of content which led to higher-than-expected acquisition across all major territories. As a result, global net adds totaled a Q2-record 5.2 million (vs. forecast of 3.2m) and increased 5% sequentially, bucking historical seasonal patterns. For the first six months of 2017, net adds are up 21% year-on-year to 10.2m.

—CEO Reed Hastings & CFO David Wells
(Netflix Q2 2017 Earnings Report)

Balancing optimistic, realistic, and strategically conservative guidance predictions of the company's quarterly performance (user growth, spending budgets, profit, and earnings, and more), forecasts have become increasingly important in maintaining the credibility of the company's now widely accepted investor lore. The rhetorical nature of economics and statistics truly shines in these earnings reports, as overperforming metrics are championed, while underperforming numbers are framed as seasonal, relative to annual growth trends and patterns, or subject to the whims of global foreign exchanges. This has never been more evident than in the most recent Netflix earnings releases such as Q1 2019, which despite a record setting quarterly addition of 9.6 million users (previously the most important indicator and corollary of stock value), the company's valuation dipped slightly. While numerous factors affect a company's stock, emergent explanations in the financial press attributed this decline in Netflix's value to a modest *forecast* for the second quarter of 2019 (Ha 2019; Rodriguez 2019). This shift indicates yet another evolution in the new temporalities of value production and projection in platform capitalism which speculate ever further into the future, negotiating narratives and timelines of risk and reward. Perhaps it is unsurprising that as competition increases, the viability and financializability of the Netflix service is ever increasingly tethered to the uncertainty of its future(s).

Indeed, with a pillar of the company's tech identity and brand advantage being its promise to anticipate, predict, and satisfy through data, the art of the forecast—setting ambitious yet deliverable goals—elucidates the cultural logic of the innovation narrative. In convergent finance and tech industries, a new (platform) capitalist fantasy emerges in which perpetually scaling growth must be maintained, and the only tools through which to do so are those of rapid innovation and perpetual engagement, in other words novelty and habit formation. Providing new products, services, and experiences are now necessary to increase market share (for more data, attention, time, revenue, and pricing power), to disrupt competition (convergence and financialization), to self-disrupt (risk, cannibalization), and lastly to merge and acquire (finding synergies of efficiency through vertical integration and consolidation of IP control). The inflationary rhetoric of such discourses and beliefs are complex and dynamic, and must be treated as such. Convergence lends itself to concentrations of media, capital, and power, through which industries are able to sustain multidirectional (vertical and/or horizontal) expansion. Perhaps the image of an umbrella is useful here, as these new hybrid tech firms are ever seeking to add and expand the reach of their many arms, and the canopy of services and products they provide: hardware, software, communication, culture, entertainment, transportation, shipping, infrastructure, banking/finance, and so on. The "+" suffix of both Apple and Disney's streaming service brands is representative of the industrial intersections of such multidirectional expansion. The brand is thus the pole of continuity holding together the umbrella of products and services; ever at the whims of global trade and finance.

> We grew annual revenue 35% to $16 billion in 2018, and nearly doubled operating profits to $1.6 billion. Fueling this growth was our high member satisfaction, which propelled us to finish 2018 with 139 million paying memberships, up 9 million from quarter start and up 29 million from the beginning of the year.
>
> —CEO Reed Hastings (Netflix 2019a, Q4 2018 Letter to Shareholders, January 17; 1)

This Q4 2018 earnings report came amidst a particularly volatile time, with the company's stock charting a drastic parabola from a summer high of over $420 per share, to a winter low of $230, and finally levelling out in mid $300s throughout the first months of 2019. Rhetorically, this report focused on annual statistics and long term projections as opposed to comparatively disappointing quarterly numbers: operating income down $216 million, operating margin down 7.5%, diluted earnings per share down from $0.89 to $0.30, and so on. While these statistics were quite close to their projected forecasts, it nonetheless demonstrates how Wall Street's enthusiasm for Netflix has recently begun to plateau, alongside of course other nebulous forces guiding the hand of the market: foreign exchange rates, seasonality, new competition, (affect driven) "bull" or "bear" markets, and most importantly the discursive negotiation of such forces and what they may hold for the future.

Where rates of subscriber growth were once enough for the finance industry to continue to bet on Netflix, 2019 brought with it a notable shift in which record setting quarters of subscriber additions no longer correlate with the drastic rises in stock value Netflix once enjoyed. Just days before Netflix's 2018 Q4 report, an article in the finance publication *The Street* hypothesized:

> Netflix is expected to have spent $13 billion on content for the full year of 2018. They have to, in order to outbid the rest of the industry for shows. This is what drives subscriber growth, and that is what—to this point—has driven share price. Not the fundamentals. The fact is that the competition for the streaming customer has only just begun. Currently, just Hulu and Amazon Prime pose a significant threat. The Walt Disney Company, Apple, and AT&T are all expected to soon raise the stakes, and in the case of Disney, the firm is already king of content. Oh, did I mention that Alphabet is also a player in the space through YouTube, and that even Walmart has expressed an interest in capturing some of these eyeballs [. . .] The stock has clearly gone parabolic since Christmas Eve on expectations for subscriber growth mixed with a likely short squeeze. Momentum has been gifted the name by the hit movie, "Bird Box." Perhaps the firm has found a way to better monetize events such as this where they find themselves with a blockbuster success on their hands. That may in fact be the real risk to short sellers right now . . . how the success of that film is discussed in the post-earnings conference call. (Guilfoyle 2019; January 15)

If efforts to explain the risk—and thus potential—of Netflix's stock and its lore, Guilfoyle highlights for the reader an increasingly large, impending wave of competition, while remaining curious as to what popular IP "events" (user experiences) like *Bird Box* might represent. Indeed the first line of Netflix's content section of the 2018 Q4 letter read "In its first 4 weeks on Netflix, we estimate that *Bird Box,* from director Susanne Bier, will be enjoyed by over 80 million member households, and we are seeing high repeat viewing." Notably, Netflix measures "one view" as "substantial completion," meaning 70 percent viewing of an episode or film, evincing the company's power to *define its own metrics*, which clearly aids the process of inflating and projecting grandiose viewership data.

Furthermore in the Q4 2018 earnings interview Sarandos stated:

> So what does it mean when 80 million households are watching—watched Bird Box? Well, culturally, it means exactly the same thing as 80 million-plus people buying a movie ticket to see it or 80 million households watching a TV show. And so culturally, it's meaningfully out there. People are talking about it, Tweeting about it, posting about it, challenging each other to do different things which we want people to be very careful when they do. But what's important is that for part of your Netflix subscription, you're in the zeitgeist. (Netflix 2019c)

This framing of Bird Box as an event or cultural moment "in the zeitgeist" evidences the company's operational logic where content experiences are published or released like tech products: phones, software updates, applications, new services, and so on. Put differently, Sarandos argues that you *need* Netflix to be an "early-adopter" of popular culture or to even participate in it. Again, Sarandos cites the *scale* and instantaneous way in which Netflix is able to wire not only hit *series* but also importantly two-hour films like *Bird Box* into millions of homes worldwide, and promote them internally on tens of millions (if not all) user homepages through "personalized" interface design and control. Indeed if a film can become a viral cultural phenomenon which powers the Netflix brand and positive user associations with the brand, then it is likely more efficient content than longer-form series in terms of buzz and the sociocultural capital associated with participating in Netflix's corners of pop culture.

THE DATA AFTER TOMORROW

Contrary to the company's famously secretive ethos surrounding streaming viewership data, this report explicitly mobilized and championed the statistical scale of the success of *Bird Box*; a show of perhaps both confidence and desperation. This twist indicates how Netflix is testing their investing audience, not unlike how they test user interfaces, to see what *other* metrics or narratives investors might positively react to and *engage with*. While this surprised many, it is actually a return to form, as the company had experimented with this format in the past, sharing top ten "most rented" lists as blog posts in the early DVD days of act one. More recently, attempts at humor such as a December 2017 tweet from Netflix's main account: "to the 53 people who have watched *A Christmas Prince* every day for the past 18 days: who hurt you?" garnered nearly 500,000 likes, and over 100,000 comments. Both blog posts and tweets such as this one exhibited to a broader audience the power of the platform to track, identify, and harness increasingly granular trends in user behavior, while also potentially raising some concerns as to the degree to which Netflix surveilles its user's behaviors (and tweets about them). As competition and uncertainty have increased for Netflix over the years, the company is now forced to negotiate the tension between the power to understand and thus theoretically provide better user experiences at the cost of surveillance. Recently, the company has begun testing a "most watched" user interface feature in UK to see what kind of "value" such data might provide users:

> Later in Q2 we'll be running a test to improve our UK member experience by releasing weekly top 10 lists of the most popular content on our UK service across various programming categories. For those who want to watch what others are watching, this may make choosing titles even easier. After a few months we'll decide whether to end or expand the test.
>
> —CEO Reed Hastings (Netflix 2019b, 4)

In an increasingly ubiquitous and competitive streaming ecology, perhaps this turn toward data sharing suggests a fourth act in Netflix's story of value.[12] Mobilizing and extolling the rhetorical power of their precious, indeed *industrially differentiating* data, the company simply cannot afford to remain as mysterious as it once had, as new industrial pressures converge upon the streaming market from Hollywood and Silicon Valley—through Wall Street. While such revelations of data remain exceptional, reserved for Netflix's biggest hits, this new aspect of the company's lore will be of particular interest in the coming quarters and years, to see how or if it is continued or expanded in any meaningful way, and if it has any positive effect for content brands, users, and/or investors.

Alongside this new exhibition of data, the Q4 2018 letter would recite and further upscale a staple of Netflix's lore, that is framing competition as one for time itself, as opposed to simply other video entertainment providers:

> In the US, we earn around 10% of television screen time[1] and less than that of mobile screen time. [. . .] We compete with (and lose to) "Fortnite" more than HBO. [. . .] There are thousands of competitors in this highly-fragmented market vying to entertain consumers and low barriers to entry for those with great experiences. Our growth is based on how good our experience is, compared to all the other screen time experiences from which consumers choose. Our focus is not

on Disney+, Amazon or others, but on how we can improve our experience for our members. [. . .] We serve on average about 100 million hours a day to television screens in the US, and we estimate television screens in the US are on about a billion hours daily (120m homes × 2 TVs × 4 hours, plus hotels, bars, etc.).

—CEO Reed Hastings, Q4 2018 Letter to Shareholders. (Netflix 2019a, 5)

As Hastings' remarked in 2007, he foresaw video gaming and YouTube as long term competitors to streaming; twelve years later, he is found beating the same drum. The incessant use of the term "experience" throughout this paragraph evidences first, how Netflix has converted TV and film into user experiences and tech products, and second, a repetitive and insistent, if not frantic, user-centric emphasis on improving their own service. In true Silicon Valley form, Netflix simultaneously boasts of achieving 100 million hours of daily domestic streaming, and yet positions this achievement as the tip of the proverbial iceberg in terms of market share. Here 10 percent suggests rather vast room for Netflix's own growth, as well as the growth of its competitors. As Netflix's *Long Term View* on its investor relations page further elaborates:

We compete for a share of members' time and spending for relaxation and stimulation, against linear networks, pay-per-view content, DVD watching, other internet networks, video gaming, web browsing, magazine reading, video piracy, and much more. Over the coming years, most of these forms of entertainment will improve. If you think of your own behavior any evening or weekend in the last month when you did not watch Netflix, you will understand how broad and vigorous our competition is. We strive to win more of our members' "moments of truth." Those decision points are, say, at 7:15 pm when a member wants to relax, enjoy a shared experience with friends and family, or is bored. The member could choose Netflix, or a multitude of other options (Netflix Investor Relations 2020).

Widening the scope of the question to that of leisure time itself, has seemingly kept investor skepticism at bay thus far, however, the majority of recent financial industry literature still cites direct competition as Netflix's biggest challenge. Perhaps this is simply *a better, more compelling story*. Only time will tell. Reflecting upon Netflix's story so far, the wide-reaching question of leisure elucidates the new, seemingly all-encompassing politicization of and *speculation upon* time in platform capitalism, wherein the quotidian practice of watching TV, in the sacred space of the home—regardless of how enjoyable, gratifying, and rewarding this may be—has itself become a highly surveilled, financialized, extractive process enabled and encouraged by our ubiquitous digital environments. The arc of the company's multifaceted discourses of user value, from the rise of DVD-by-mail, to streaming, to massive transnational original programming efforts, have culminated in the unprecedented scale of and competition for platform tv today. Hastings is correct when he says there has never been more content being produced; similarly there has never been more capital circulated so quickly. As culture and tech industries converge through finance; this has been, and will continue to be no coincidence.

Another notable turn toward greater information sharing and forecasting in Netflix's investor lore has been the new regional breakdowns and predictions of user acquisition, revenue, and average-revenue-per-user (ARPU) as of January 2020. In the company's Q4 2019 investor letter, the globe was divided into four categories "Asia Pacific (APAC), Europe, Middle East & Africa (EMEA), Latin America (LATAM), and the United States and Canada (UCAN). UCAN is roughly 90% US and 10% Canada" (Netflix 2019f). As Netflix's non-domestic growth constitutes an ever greater majority of its user base, this shift to provide greater regional context indicates the desire or perhaps necessity for Netflix's investors to know *where* the company is growing, and how profitable each region is to the company. This desire for finer regional detail has been evident in Netflix's earnings calls for years, as investors frequently asked the company's executives for country and region-specific data (Netflix 2017b; Netflix 2018c; Netflix 2019b). This new facet of Netflix's lore will certainly be of interest to watch in the coming years, as it will provide Netflix's executives and investors with greater opportunities to discuss how, where, and in part *why* Netflix is focusing its expansion efforts.

> Fellow shareholders, We had a strong finish to 2019, with Q4 revenue growing 31% year over year, bringing full year 2019 revenue to over $20 billion, while FY19 operating income rose 62% to $2.6 billion. During the quarter, we surpassed 100 million paid memberships outside of the US. Streaming entertainment is a global phenomenon and we're working hard to build on our early progress.
>
> —CEO Reed Hastings, Q4 2019 Letter to Shareholders, January 21, 2020
> (Netflix 2020).

The historical numbers touted here entice the reader to associate them with Netflix's entire history, strategy, and identity as a company. Emphasizing scaled growth over time, this quote frames the company's temporalities and projections of current and, therefore, future value. Beneath this positive message, however, lies the company's remaining dependence upon investors. The journey of Netflix's stock value over the past few years has become increasingly erratic, bouncing around anywhere and everywhere from a low of $196.10 in January 2018 to a peak of $575.37 in mid-July 2020. The subsequent fluctuations of tens of billions of dollars in market capitalization during this year speaks, again, to the ever inflationary stakes in the choose your own adventure gam(bl)e of finance (Macrotrends 2020). Our narrators are always less reliable, or at least much less omniscient, then we think. With this we can see how *forecasts* are being given increasing weight, to balance out the fantasy narrative of endless subscriber additions and revenue. As fantasies of endless growth are supplanted by mythologies of projection, which is really the deeper abstraction?

Since Netflix's Q1 2019 report, there has been greater emphasis placed upon projections and forecasting, as record setting subscriber additions and revenues have been met with slight dips in stock value, attributed, again, to low growth forecasts for following quarters, as well as the launch of various competitors throughout 2019 and 2020: Apple TV+, Disney+, HBOMax, and Comcast/NBCUniversal's Peacock. As Netflix's story of value becomes increasingly tethered not only to performance statistics but more importantly to the *projection of statistics*, we can see how the company and its figureheads are seeking to rhetorically compensate for this shift; attempting, more than ever before, to scale their discourses in efforts to sustain the belief and investment necessary to sustain the power and growth of the Netflix brand —as a service and a stock. If Wall Street's faith in Netflix's future wanes, the company's ability to access capital and other instruments of global finance (massive debt markets, bonds, post-IPO funding rounds, stock buy-backs, etc.) will be importantly diminished. Netflix heavily depends upon such mechanisms and flows of capital to maintain its ever-expanding "global" operations and programming, but if the lore fails, if the story of value ceases to compel, investors—like users—may cancel their subscriptions, threatening the sustainability of the central project of the Netflix as we have come to know it.

POST-CREDIT SEQUENCE

In the first two financial quarters of the COVID-19 pandemic, tech stocks have weathered stormy markets, and in many cases profited greatly. It is no surprise that the two companies most associated with staying at home— Netflix and Amazon—have seen the greatest benefits throughout the global lockdown. Netflix added 15.5M new subscribers in Q1 2020, and another 10.1M in Q2 2020, closing in on the 27.8M it added in all of 2019. Such numbers were met with initial optimism from the investing market, sending the Netflix stock drastically upward to heights of $575 in mid-July, but predictably tapering off with the company's publication of a low forecast of 2.5M subscriber additions for Q3 2020. This ebb and flow of emotion, investment, and prediction speaks to the gambling effect of finance itself. Pulled in by both the allure and the brutality of uncertainty, the investing class manages their portfolios, waiting to see who benefits and who perishes; to see which of their "feelings" or predictions were correct, but what COVID lays bare, is just how much is truly beyond our control or anticipation. It may have been known that a global pandemic was inevitable, but no one knew just when, or how severe, or what effects it may have; in essence all the vitally important and meaningful details remained unknown and unpredicted.

While shelter-in-place and social-distancing measures are being slowly lifted (or blatantly ignored), it is still uncertain as to how long the pandemic and its effects will last. How will such measures affect the content production of Netflix and film and television industries more broadly? These are all questions at the tops of the minds of media executives and investors the world over; after all time is money. What is observable, however, is that the pandemic has only seemed to exacerbate preexisting trends in the media industries: increasing digital media consumption and communication, increasingly remote and fragmented digital labor, increasing e-commerce and delivery services: amazon prime and food delivery, and so on. Our digital lifestyles have been accelerated by COVID, and it is very unclear what the world may look like if or when "this is over" but it seems that many of these digital trends are here to stay.

Structurally, Netflix named Chief Content Officer Ted Sarandos co-CEO in its latest quarterly report, with Hastings commenting "Ted has been my partner for decades. This change makes formal what was already informal— that Ted and I share the leadership of Netflix" (Netflix 2020b). While this announcement seemed to have little effect in the financial press, tech and entertainment publications discussed how the move signals the increasing importance of Netflix's identity as a film and television studio, as well as hinting at long term succession planning for the company's leadership (Jenkins 2020; Spangler 2020). In the quarterly earnings call, Hastings made clear that he was "in it for another decade" and that Sarandos' promotion is easily deserved given his accomplishments and leadership in his twenty year tenure at the company. Only time will tell what the symbolic sharing of the role of CEO and thus chief narrator will bring for the company, but in the meantime, it indicates Hastings' desire to retire (in ten years apparently) and his hopes for a smooth and gradual transition out of the company. What the platform TV industry looks like in 2030, however, is truly anyone's guess.

NOTES

1. See Ramon Lobato's *Netflix Nations* (2019) for an in-depth critique of the vastly uneven geographies and experiences of Netflix.

2. The Nielsen rating system attempts to monitor representative cross section of television consumers and markets, through selecting families and households as sample groups, known as Nielsen households (Nielsen 2019).

3. See Finn's 2017 book "What Algorithms Want: Chapter 3 The Aesthetics of Abstraction" for more detail on micro-genre tags and Netflix's algorithmic production information.

4. Thanks to Dr. Elena Pnevmonidou for pointing me in the direction of Goethe's World Literature.

5. See Finn's "What Algorithms Want" (2017) for more on computational rationality.

6. "This year we expect to offer our members over 600 hours of high quality original programming from some of the world's most talented people, and the only place you'll find it is on Netflix [. . .] With the internet, global distribution no longer needs to be fragmented. It means that everyone pretty much everywhere should be able to see great films and TV shows at the exact same moment" (Sarandos, CES 2016).

7. Facebook COO Sheryl Sandberg has declared Netflix's "Culture Deck" slideshow one of the most important documents to come out of Silicon Valley, furthering the documents already wide circulation in tech industry human relations (Fernstein 2013).

8. Pages 14–17 in literature review for Lotz's affordances of nonlinear TV.

9. See Burroughs 2018; Jenner 2015; 2016; McCracken 2013; Matrix 2014.

10. See Kevin Spacey's 2014 James Mactaggart Memorial Lecture at the Edinburgh Television Festival, for example.

11. Mark Zuckerberg's infamous motto for "disruptive innovation" at Facebook.

12. "For Q1'19, in scripted English language TV, we premiered another big hit in 'Umbrella Academy,' based on the comic book by Gerard Way and Gabriel Bá, which has been watched by 45 million member households in its first four weeks on service. Our original films effort built on the momentum from our Q4 blockbuster 'Bird Box' with 'Triple Frontier,' starring Ben Affleck and directed by J.C. Chandor. This action/heist movie has been watched by over 52 million member households in its first four weeks on Netflix. 'The Highwaymen' (starring Kevin Costner and Woody Harrelson as two lawmen that bring Bonnie and Clyde to justice) is on track to being watched by over 40 million member households in its first month" (Netflix Letter to Shareholders, Q1 2019 [2019, April 16; 3]).

Coda

Since its inception, Netflix and its narrators have been constructing the speculative fictions of its investor lore, effectively branding the company as a disruptive, innovative, and resilient player in the technology, culture, and finance industries of both the past and the future. The company's first two acts constructed a narrative of collaboration with consumer electronics companies and content owners in fostering the media ecosystems of DVD and later Smart TVs and streaming. The affordances of these convergent digital technologies allowed Netflix to both project and provide the unparalleled convenience of these new user experiences, disrupting the brick and mortar retail model of video rental with DVD-rental-by-mail, and eventually "disrupting itself" with the shift to streaming; bringing TV fully online. Crafting and *selling* this teleology of an inevitable and thus potentially valuable future market of platform TV, Netflix and its market valuation has seen explosive growth since the late 2000s, with audiences of users and investors alike glued to their screens. Central throughout these processes has been the company's ability to extract increasingly intricate behavioral user data, and mobilize such data to inform each aspect of its operations. This was true of the DVD days, and remains so today in the era of the "Netflix Global Original."

Focusing on international market expansion, Netflix has grown its user base to nearly 193 million, and as of the final draft of this book in mid-2020, its market capitalization has been hovering around $215 billion. This valuation of just over $1,100/per user speaks to the inflated speculative fictions of Netflix and the financialization of platform television; a fiction that could implode should Netflix's lore begin to fail. Of course Netflix's other assets factor into this overall market capitalization, including $7.2B in cash assets, $25B in content assets, $2.7B in "non-current assets" (other not yet realized investments, long term assets, intellectual property, patents), and $650M in property and equipment. However, these assets are also counterbalanced in part by the company's $27.8B total long term debts and liabilities. The cashflow juggling act of revenue, capital, and debt in Netflix's financial documents is at the end of the day sustained by its successful investor lore; by language. The affectual bonds the financial community shares with Netflix maintain its inflated valuation and the financial power that affords, namely its ability to access debt markets and capital at staggering scales. What the story of Netflix has shown is that the hybrid techno-culture industry of platform television is built upon such structures of debt and financialization and their attendant ideas about the future; but are such visions of the future promises or threats?

The techno-liberal ideology of Netflix and its lore elucidates these new narratives and logics of value in a deeply and complexly developed information age. As Nick Srnicek notes in *Platform Capitalism*, the logic of the platform economy is inherently monopolistic, exacerbating and accelerating concentrations of capital and power, as aggressive attempts to grow usership and market share are prioritized over immediate profitability (2017, 54, 93). Among its tech-based competitors, Netflix remains exceptionally singular in its focus. This company sparked the industrial race for virtually every major tech and entertainment conglomerate to converge upon the market of platform TV in some capacity, and streaming dominance remains Netflix's only goal—albeit on an ambitiously international scale. For example, Amazon offers Prime Video as an addendum to their e-commerce and cloud computing empire. Apple TV+ is one of many new Apple *services* and subscriptions hoping to mediate declining *product* sales. Google (YouTube) and Facebook seek to extract new value from video content on their social platforms, largely through targeted advertising, as well as small paid subscription and rental models. As far as we know, Netflix is not reaching out into the spheres of consumer electronics, e-commerce, hardware, or targeted advertising; instead, the company claims to remain focused solely on furthering their narrative as "the world's leading internet entertainment service," a "global" TV studio *and* network, innovating the way stories are told and shared. Netflix's most successful, valuable, and innovative program thus far is the lore of Netflix itself, the culmination of a two-decade project of participatory storytelling; a metanarrative of value; a speculative fiction. On the content and entertainment industry side, where Netflix once famously aspired to be HBO; HBO, Disney, Comcast, AT&T, and even the Criterion Collection have been forced to *become Netflix* as its streaming platform model has become increasingly popular and increasingly valuable.

Returning to Jameson's idea that the flows of finance capitalism will always be reflected in and by mass culture industries, Netflix and its new media economics provide a compelling case study through which to analyze such processes. Netflix's guiding logics of flexibility, scale, surveillance, and debt all speak to the broader structures and movements of labor, capital, culture, and value in today's platform economies. Each of these processes—financing, distribution, promotion, and consumption of internet film and television–are driven by platform capitalism's narratives, assemblages, and flows of value: data, time, attention, capital, information, infrastructure, code, labor, sociality, and so on. For the investor, the question arises: how will these new forms and processes produce returns on my investment in near or distant futures? "Talent"—workers creating code or content alike—asks: Will our *products* reach, engage, and impact users and their ever more important *experiences?* And finally, users are subjected to more "choice" and speculation than ever before: which platform, which subscription, which show(s), which film(s), which ratings, which recommendations, which screen, which device, which internet provider, and so on. (Com) Promises of quality, quantity, popularity, affordability—of cultural, social, and economic capital—push and pull valuable users ever across the stage of platform capitalism. Where each brand tells its own story, they all abide by the conventions of finance's speculative fictions; each beholden to their own investor lore as the site of communicating value, capital, influence, and power. As culture becomes increasingly digital, algorithmic, and financial, it also becomes increasingly speculative. Today's temporalities of value generation mobilize ever greater debts and ever faster exchanges, channeling profits into the hands of a shrinking few, and casting value ever further into the future.

Through the nurturing of a ubiquitous platform ecology for televisual and filmic consumption over the internet, Netflix has foregrounded the potential value of monitoring and measuring each aspect of a user's behavior on the platform, extracting each moment of attention and interaction into an investment of data, the raw material of the new economy. For over twenty years, the narrators of Netflix's investor lore have consistently put forth a narrative with relatable characters: *users, investors,* and *"talent";* a conflict or problem which their innovation can resolve: *the neoliberal solutionism of disruption and market creation*; compelling story arcs: *risk, investment, debt, scale, competition, profit*; and the finally implication of a happily ever after: *the capitalist fantasy of perpetual profit, scale, and growth, perhaps ending in monopolization through vertical integration, concentration, and conglomeration.* The adoption of this narrative has fundamentally reshaped media industries, as the datafication, and in turn financialization of watching, speaks not only to the model of Netflix but rather our expanding platform economy writ large. One must *engage*—navigate, click, look, listen, share, mention, and discuss—to participate in any digital cultural form, exchanging not only one's capital but their very *behavior* for access.

These stories of value in platform capitalism are mobilized to inspire faith in *data*, perpetuating the perceived potentiality of power and profitability. When this story compels, it compels billions of dollars of investment, and billions of hours of attention. The emergent constellations of technology, culture, and finance today elucidate the convergent drive of platform capitalism to harness the power of our digital environments to monitor, measure, mobilize human behaviors and practices of everyday life. While the increasing number of streaming platforms today suggests heightened competition, one can only imagine a wave of mergers, acquisitions, and bundles will surely follow this initial surge of streaming platforms into the market. The coming years will no doubt bring about new narratives of value as these major media platforms—now all industrial hybrids of culture, technology, and finance—race for intellectual property, content, infrastructure, and of course *users*. The distances between Silicon Valley, Hollywood, and Wall Street are shrinking. As television increasingly becomes a *user experience*, it also in turn becomes a financial technology.

Our digital languages, from C++ to executive discourses, from Google to Goldman Sachs, now bind our exchanges of data, capital, and culture through the converging infrastructures of global finance and technology. The state of media industries indicate how the new financializing logics and processes of platformization are now subsuming contemporary cultural production: in Hollywood studios, movie theatres, living room screens, and on mobile phones. This book has offered a narrative analysis of these logics, discourses, and processes through the example of Netflix, a leader in the convergent media industry of platform TV. What I have hoped to show here is that the uncertainty and risk of today's unprecedented scales and speeds of cultural production are prefigured by the financializing narratives of value upon which Silicon Valley has been built.

This genre of speculative fiction thrives upon narratives of prediction, automation, artificial intelligence, and sentient machines; negotiating, exploring, and projecting the *value* of human life and experience, right to its bleeding edges. While these new forms and flows of value may be accelerated and automated through machine learning, high-frequency algorithmic trading, and algorithmically filtered recommendations; technologies, markets, and audiences are (for now) still largely created by and for *people*. As long as humans are writing, buying, and investing in the narratives of value which organize these processes, it will remain that people will always require others to map and understand these flows and forms; to hypothesize and speculate upon their effects; and ultimately of course to exchange these new embodiments of digital value. Such acceleration and automation removes many people and their labor from such processes, and concentrates capital, information, and power into the hands of an elite few, who must provide narratives to justify and organize such imbalances. These are the stories we must understand, unpack, and resist.

All that is solid melts into air, condensates in the cloud, streams down, and evaporates once more. These are the "real conditions of life, and relations with our kind" which we must compel ourselves and each other to face (Marx and Engels 1848, 4). It simply doesn't have to be this way.

This life of convergence is fundamentally one of storytelling, language, feeling, and relation, wherein new choreographies of value and power are pushed, pulled, negotiated, narrativized through a new political, economic, and cultural stage; a new platform (of) capitalism. It is absolutely vital that we understand and reorganize the concentrations of capital that the internet is accelerating into radically imaginative, public, and redistributive forms. Our work now is to create and write our own speculative fictions, based not upon capital accumulation and power, but rather inclusive social and public values, accessibility, and resilience.

Bibliography

Abkowitz, Alyssa. 2009. "How Netflix got started." *Fortune*. January 28, 2009. http://fortune.com

Alexander, Julia. 2017. "Netflix is going to be fine, even with a $20 billion debt and a Disney-less future." *Polygon*. August 15, 2017. http://polyglon.com

Amatriain, Xavier. 2013. Big & personal: Data and models behind Netflix recommendations. BigMine'13: Proceedings of the 2nd International Workshop on Big Data, streams and heterogeneous Source Mining: Algorithms, systems, programming models and applications. August 2013. 1–6. DOI: 10.1145/2501221.2501222.

Appadurai, Arjun. 2015. *Banking on words: The failure of language in the age of derivative finance*. Chicago: University of Chicago Press.

Arango, Tim. 2010. "Times warner views Netflix as a fading star." *The New York Times*. December 12, 2010. http://nytimes.com

Austin, John Langshaw. 1962. *How to do things with words*. New York: Oxford University Press.

Baumer, Eric, and Jed R. Brubaker. 2017. "Post-userism." CHI '17: Proceedings of the 2017 CHI Conference on Human Factors in Computing Systems. May 2017. 6291–6303. DOI: 10.1145/3025453.3025740

Bond, Paul. 2011. "Netflix outbids HBO for David Fincher and Kevin Spacey's 'House of Cards.'" *The Hollywood Reporter*. March 15, 2011. http://hollywood-reporter.com

Bingham, John. 2012. "TV drama is the new literature, says Salman Rushdie." *The Telegraph*. June 12, 2011. http://telegraph.co.uk

Burroughs, Benjamin. 2018. "House of Netflix: Streaming media and digital lore." *Popular Communication* 17(1), 1–17.

Caldwell, John. 2006. "Chapter 5: Cultural studies of media production: Critical industrial practices." in *Questions of method in Cultural Studies*, edited by Mimi White and James Schwoch, pp. 109–153. Malden: Wiley-Blackwell.

Callon, Michel. 2007. "What does it mean to say that economics is performative?" in *Do economists make markets? On the performativity of economics*, edited by

Donald A. MacKenzie, Fabian Muniesa, and Lucia Siu, pp. 311–357. Princeton: Princeton University Press.

Chmielewski, Dawn C. 2013. "Netflix executive upends Hollywood." *Los Angeles Times*. August 25, 2013. http://latimes.com

Chun, Wendy Hui Kyong. 2016. *Updating to remain the same: Habitual New Media.* Cambridge: MIT press.

Citton, Yves. 2017. *The ecology of attention.* Translated by Barnaby Norman. Cambridge: Polity.

Copeland, Michael V. 2010. "Reed hastings: Leader of the pack." *Fortune*. November 18, 2010. http://fortune.com

Crunchbase. 2019. "Netflix - funding rounds." Last modified 2019. http://crunchbase .com

Currie, Wendy L., and Thomas Lagoarde-Segot. 2017. "Financialization and information technology: themes, issues and critical debates–part I." *Journal of Information Technology* 32, 211–217.

Curtin, Michael, Jennifer Holt, and Kevin Sanson. *Distribution Revolution: Conversations about the Digital Future of Film and Television.* University of California Press, 2014.

Davis, Gerald F., and Suntae Kim. 2015. "Financialization of the economy." *Annual Review of Sociology* 41, 203–221.

Eckermann, Johann Peter. 2011. *Conversations of Goethe with Eckermann and Soret.* Translated by John Oxenford, vol. 1. London: Cambridge University Press.

The Economist. 2019. "The wave of unicorn IPOs reveals Silicon Valley's groupthink: There is more to life than blitzscaling." April 17, 2019. http://economist.com

Elliot, Megan. 2019. "You won't believe how many original movies and shows Netflix released in 2019." *Showbiz Cheatsheet*. December 25, 2019. http://cheatsheet.com

Faltesek, Daniel. 2018. *Selling Social Media: The Political Economy of Social Networking.* Bloomsbury Publishing USA.

Fernstein, Gregory. 2013. "Read what Facebook's Sandberg calls maybe 'The most important document ever to come out of the Valley.'" *TechCrunch*. January 31, 2013. http://techcrunch.com

Fidler, Roger. 1997. *Mediamorphosis: Understanding New Media.* Thousand Oaks: Pine Forge Press.

Finn, Ed. 2017. *What Algorithms Want: Imagination in the age of computing.* Cambridge: MIT Press.

Garcia, Feliks. 2015. "How Adam Sandler became an unlikely Latin American comedy icon." *Complex Magazine*. November 20, 2015. http://complex.com

Golumbia, David. 2009. *The Cultural Logic of computation.* Cambridge: Harvard University Press.

GreaterThanX. 2017. "To design digital experiences that matter, design for the 5 Senses." GreaterThanX. March 24, 2017. *Medium*. http://medium.com

Greene, Andy. 2013. "How Lilyhammer changed the TV World." *Rolling Stone*. December 5, 2013. http://rollingstone.com

Grinapol, Corinne. 2013. *Reed Hastings and Netflix.* The Rosen Publishing Group, Inc.

Griswold, A. 2019. "Famously unprofitable Amazon has nothing on Uber." *Quartz.* April 11, 2019. Retrieved from http://qz.com

Ha, Anthony. 2019. "Netflix added 9.6M subscribers in Q1, with revenue of $4.5B." *TechCrunch.* April 16, 2019. Retrieved from http://techcrunch.com

Hallinan, Blake, and Ted Striphas. 2016. "Recommended for you: The Netflix Prize and the production of algorithmic culture." *New media & society* 18(1), 117–137.

Hass, Nancy. 2013. "Is Netflix the next HBO?" *GQ.* January 29, 2013. http://gq.com

Havens, Tim. 2008. *The evolution of industry lore in African American television trade.*
Montreal: International Communications Association.

Havens, Tim 2014. Towards a structuration theory of media intermediaries. in *Making Media Work: Cultures of management in the entertainment industries,* edited by Derek Johnson, Derek Kompare, and Avi Santo, pp. 39–62. New York: NYU Press.

Hawkins, Andrew J. 2018. "Uber reportedly lost $891 million in the second quarter of 2018 as growth Slows. *The Verge.* August 15, 2018. http://theverge.com

Holt, Jenn. 2017. *Cloud Policy: Anatomy of a Regulatory Crisis.* Lecture Presentation at Concordia University, Global Emergent Media Lab. October 30, 2017.

Hyland, Ken. 1998. "Exploring corporate rhetoric: Metadiscourse in the CEO's letter." *The Journal of Business Communication 1973* 35(2), 224–244.

Jameson, Fredric. 1997. "Culture and finance capital." *Critical Inquiry* 24(1), 246–265.

Jenkins, Aric. 2020. "Ted Sarandos was already co-CEO of Netflix." *Fortune.* July 17 2020. http://fortune.com

Jenkins, Henry. 2006. *Convergence culture: where old and new Media Collide.* New York: New York University Press.

Jenner, Mareike. 2016. "Is this TVIV? On Netflix, TVIII and binge-watching." *New media & society* 18(2), 257–273.

Jenner, Mareike. 2017. "Binge-watching: Video-on-demand, quality TV and main-streaming Fandom." *International Journal of Cultural Studies* 20(3), 304–320.

Jenner, Mareike. 2018. *Netflix and the Re-invention of Television.* Springer.

Johnson, Derek, Derek Kompare, and Avi Santo, eds. 2014. *Making Media Work: cultures of management in the Entertainment Industries.* NYU Press.

Knee, Jonathan A., Bruce C. Greenwald, and Ava Seave. 2009. *The curse of the mogul: What's wrong with the world's Leading Media Companies.* New York: Penguin.

Kujala, Sari, Virpi Roto, Kaisa Väänänen-Vainio-Mattila, Evangelos Karapanos, and Arto Sinnelä. 2011. "UX Curve: A method for evaluating long-term user experience." *Interacting with computers* 23(5), 473–483.

Leigh, Danny. 2017. "David Fincher on his new Netflix series Mindhunter and what's gone wrong with filmmaking." *Financial Times.* October 12, 2017. http://ft.com

Lobato, Ramon. 2017. *Geographies of Streaming.* Keynote Presentation at Porting Media II Conference, Concordia University, October 14, 2017.

Lobato, Ramon. 2018. "Rethinking international TV flows research in the age of Netflix." *Television & New Media* 19(3), 241–256.

Lobato, Ramon. 2019. *Netflix nations: the geography of Digital Distribution*. New York: NYU Press.

Loudenback, Terry. 2015. "Meet Reed Hastings, the man who built Netflix." *Business Insider*. September 6, 2015. http://businessinsider.com

Lotz, Amanda D. 2014. *The television will be revolutionized*. New York: NYU Press.

Lotz, Amanda D. 2014. "Building theories of creative industry managers: challenges, perspectives, and future directions." In *Making Media Work: Cultures of Management in the Entertainment Industries*. Eds. Derek Johnson, Derek Kompare, and Avi Santo. Vol. 17, pp. 25–38. NYU Press.

Lotz, Amanda D. 2015. "Assembling a toolkit." *Media Industries* 1(3), 18–21.

Lotz, Amanda D. 2017. *Portals: A treatise on Internet-Distributed Television*. Ann Arbor: Maize Books.

Lubin, Gus. 2016. "How Netflix will someday know exactly what you want to watch as soon as you turn your TV on." *Business Insider*. September 25, 2016. http://businenessinsider.com

Lury, Celia. 2004. *Brands: The logos of the Global Economy*. Routledge.

Macrotrends. "Netflix Market Cap 2006-2019." 2020. Macrotrends. Last modified 2020. http://macrotrends.com

Marx, Karl, and Friedrich Engels. 2002 [1848]. *The Communist Manifesto*. Translated by Sam Moore. Penguin, 2002.

Matrix, Sidneyeve. 2014. "The Netflix effect: Teens, binge watching, and on-demand digital media trends." *Jeunesse: Young People, Texts, Cultures* 6(1), 119–138.

Maynard, John. 2004. "With DVD, TV viewers can channel their choices." *The Washington Post*. January 30, 2004. http://washingtonpost.com

McAlone, Nathan. 2016. "Cable TV price increases have beaten inflation every single year for 20 years." *Business Insider*. October 31, 2016. http://businessinsider.com

McCracken, Grant. 2013. "Arrested development to doctor who, Binge-watching is changing our culture." *Wired*. May 24, 2013. http://wired.com

McDonald, Kevin, and Daniel Smith-Rowsey, eds. 2016. *The Netflix effect: Technology and entertainment in the 21st century*. Bloomsbury Publishing.

Morgan, Blake. 2016. "Netflix and late fees: How consumer-centric companies are changing the tide." *Forbes*. October 7, 2016. http://forbes.com

Negroponte, Nicholas. 1995. *Being Digital*. New York: Random House.

Netflix. 1998a. Netflix Press Release. http://media.netflix.com

Netflix. 1998b. Netflix Press Release. http://media.netflix.com

Netflix. 1998c. Netflix Press Release. http://media.netflix.com

Netflix. 1999. Netflix Press Release. http://media.netflix.com

Netflix. 2000. Netflix Press Release. http://media.netflix.com

Netflix. 2002. 2002 Annual Report. https://www.netflixinvestor.com/

Netflix. 2003. 2003 Annual Report. https://www.netflixinvestor.com/

Netflix. 2004. 2004 Annual Report. https://www.netflixinvestor.com/

Netflix. 2005. 2005 Annual Report. https://www.netflixinvestor.com/

Netflix. 2006. 2006 Annual Report. https://www.netflixinvestor.com/

Netflix. 2007. 2007 Annual Report. https://www.netflixinvestor.com

Netflix. 2008. 2008 Annual Report. https://www.netflixinvestor.com/

Netflix. 2008a. Netflix Press Release. http://media.netflix.com

Netflix. 2008b. Netflix Press Release. http://media.netflix.com

Netflix. 2010. 2010 Third Quarter Letter to Shareholders. https://www.netflixinvest or.com.com/results.cfmf

Netflix. 2011. 2010 Fourth Quarter Letter to Shareholders. http://media.netflix.com

Netflix. 2011a. 2011 Third Quarter Earnings Call Transcript. https://www.netflixin-vestor.com/

Netflix. 2011b. 2011 First Quarter Letter to Shareholders. https://www.netflixinvestor .com/

Netflix. 2012. 2012 First Quarter Letter to Shareholders. https://www.netflixinvestor .com/

Netflix. 2013. 2013 First Quarter Letter to Shareholders. https://www.netflixinvestor .com/

Netflix. 2016, Jan 6. Netflix CES 2016 Keynote | Reed Hastings, Ted Sarandos – Full Length. http://youtube.com/netflix

Netflix. 2016a. First Quarter Earnings Call Transcript. April 18, 2016. https://www .netflixinvestor.com/

Netflix. 2017. 2016 Fourth Quarter Letter to Shareholders. January 18, 2017. https:// www.netflixinvestor.com/

Netflix. 2017a. 2017 Third Quarter Letter to Shareholders. October 16, 2017. https:// www.netflixinvestor.com/

Netflix. 2017b. Netflix Q3 2017 Earnings Interview. *Netflix Investor Relations YouTube Channel.* Oct 16, 2017. http://youtube.com

Netflix. 2018. 2017 Fourth Quarter Letter to Shareholders. https://www.netflixinves-tor.com/

Netflix. 2018a. 2018 First Quarter Letter to Shareholders. https://www.netflixinvestor .com/

Netflix. 2018b. 2018 Second Quarter Letter to Shareholders. https://www.netflixin-vestor.com/

Netflix. 2018c. 2018 Third Quarter Letter to Shareholders. https://www.netflixinves-tor.com/

Netflix. 2019. Netflix Investor Relations. http://netflixinvestor.com

Netflix. 2019a. 2018 Fourth Quarter Letter to Shareholders. https://www.netflixinves-tor.com/

Netflix. 2019b. 2018 Fourth Quarter Earnings Call Transcript. https://www.netflix-investor.com/

Netflix. 2019c. 2019 First Quarter Letter to Shareholders. https://www.netflixinvestor .com/

Netflix. 2019d. 2019 Second Quarter Letter to Shareholders. https://www.netflixin-vestor.com/

Netflix. 2019e. 2019 Third Quarter Letter to Shareholders. https://www.netflixinves-tor.com/

Netflix. 2020. 2019 Fourth Quarter Letter to Shareholders. https://www.netflixinves-tor.com/

Netflix. 2020a. 2020 First Quarter Letter to Shareholders. https://www.netflixinvestor.com/

Netflix. 2020b. 2020 Second Quarter Letter to Shareholders. https://www.netflixinvestor.com

Netflix Investor Relations 2020. Netflix Investor Relations – Long Term View. https://www.netflixinvestor.com/

Netflix Media Center. 2011. Blog Post - Ted Sarandos http://media.netflix.com

Netflix Media Center. 2011a. "An Explanation and Some Reflections." Netflix Media Blog. http://media.netflix.com

Netflix Media Center. 2016. Netflix Media Center Website. http://media.netflix.com

Netflix Media Center. 2017 Aug 13. "Shonda Rhimes and Shondaland come to Netflix." http://media.netflix.com

Netflix Tech Blog 2016; 2017 Netflix Tech Blog Website. http://medium.com/netflix-techblog

Nielsen Company 2019. "Nielsen TV + Radio Ratings and Nielsen Families." http://nielsen.com

Nocera, Joe. 2016. "Can Netflix survive in a world it created?" *The New York Times.* June 15, 2016. http://nytimes.com

Ovide, Shira. 2018. "Let's get real about Netflix's numbers." *Bloomberg Business.* April 16, 2018. http://bloomberg.com

Orlin, Jon. 2010. "Internet TV and The Death of Cable TV, really." *Tech Crunch.* October 24, 2010. http://techcrunch.com

Perez, Sarah. 2017. "Netflix and HBO cleaned up at the Emmys." *Tech Crunch.* September 18, 2017. http://techcrunch.com

Perzanowski, Aaron, and Jason Schultz. 2016. *The end of ownership: Personal property in the Digital Economy.* MIT Press.

Pollak, Sally. 2015. "Netflix tight-lipped on audience statistics. *USA Today.*" March 13, 2015. http://usatoday.com

Plaugic, Lizzie. 2017. "David Letterman is leaving retirement to host a Netflix series." *The Verge.* March 13, 2017. http://theverge.com

Prange, Stephanie. 2020. "Study: Netflix Launched nine times as much original programming as Amazon in 2019." *Media Play News.* March 17, 2020. http://mediaplaynews.com

Rogowsky, Mark. 2011. "What are the most notable aspects of Netflix's Q3 2011 Earnings Report?" *Quora.* October 25, 2011. http://quora.com

Rodriguez, Ashley. 2017. "Netflix was founded 20 years ago today because Reed Hastings was late returning a video." *Quartz.* August 29, 2017. http://quartz.com

Rodriguez, Ashley. 2019. "Keeping up with Netflix originals is basically a part-time job now." *Quartz.* January 1, 2019. http://quartz.com

Rodriguez, Ashley. 2019. "Netflix slides after beating Q1 subscriber growth estimates but giving weak guidance for the months ahead." *Business Insider.* April 16, 2019. Retrieved from http://businessinsider.com

Santo, Avi. 2009. "Para-television and discourses of distinction: The culture of production at HBO." In *It's Not TV*, pp. 31–57. Routledge.

Sauer, Patrick J. 2005. "How I Did It: Reed Hastings, Netflix." *Inc.* December 1, 2005. http://www.inc.com

Sebastien, Michael. 2014. "Did wired just create the 'Snowfall' of native advertising for Netflix?" *AdAge.* May 15, 2014. http://adage.com

Segal, Tony. 2020, May 4. Enron Scandal: The fall of a wall street darling. *Investopedia.* Retrieved from http://investopedia.com

Setoodeh, Ramin. 2017. "Has Netflix's Ted Sarandos rescued or ruined Hollywood? *Variety.* August 15, 2017. http://variety.com

Sietz, Patrick. 2017. "Netflix fall continues over end of Disney movie deal." *Investors Business Daily.* August 10, 2017. http://investors.com

Sim, Gerald. 2016. "Individual disruptors and economic gamechangers: Netflix, new media, and neoliberalism." in *The Netflix Effect: Technology and Entertainment in the 21ˢᵗ Century*, edited by Kevin McDonald, and Daniel Smith-Rowsey, pp. 185–201. New York: Bloomsbury.

Smith, Craig. 2018. "110 Amazing Netflix statistics and facts August 2018." *Digital Marketing Ramblings.* August 12, 2018. http://expandedramblings.com

Smith, Michael D., and Rahul Telang. 2016. *Streaming, sharing, stealing: Big Data and the future of entertainment.* Cambridge: MIT Press.

Spangler, Todd. 2017. "Apple Sets $1 billion budget for original TV shows, movies (report)." *Variety.* August 16, 2017. http://variety.com

Spangler, Todd. 2018. "Netflix eyeing total of about 700 original series in 2018." *Variety.* February 27, 2018. http://variety.com

Spangler, Todd. 2020. "Ted Sarandos named Netflix Co-CEO alongside reed hastings." *Variety.* July 17 2020. http://variety.com

Srnicek, Nick. 2016. *Platform Capitalism.* Cambridge: Polity Press.

Statista 2020. "Leading reasons why Netflix subscribers in the U.S. subscribed to Netflix as of January 2015"; data reported in eMarketer a Cowan & Company study, methodology not specified. Last modified 2020. http://www.statista.com/s tatistics/459906/reasons-subscribe-netflix-usa/.

Steinberg, Marc. 2012. *Anime's Media Mix: Franchising toys and characters in Japan.* Minneapolis: University of Minnesota Press.

Steinberg, Marc. 2019. *The Platform Economy: How Japan Transformed the Consumer Internet.* Minneapolis: University of Minnesota Press.

Terranova, Tiziana. 2004. *Network Culture: Cultural Politics for the Information Age.* Pluto Press.

Tryon, Chuck. 2009. *Reinventing cinema: Movies in the age of Media Convergence.* New Brunswick: Rutgers University Press.

Tryon, Chuck. 2015. "TV got better: Netflix's original programming strategies and the on-demand television transition." *Media Industries Journal* 2(2), 104–116.

Tsing, Anna. 2009. "Supply chains and the human condition." *Rethinking Marxism* 21(2), 148–176.

Van Alstyne, Marshall W., Geoffrey G. Parker, and Sangeet Paul Choudary. 2016. "Pipelines, platforms, and the new rules of strategy." *Harvard Business Review* 94(4), 54–62.

Van den Boomen, Marianne V. 2014. *Transcoding the digital: How Metaphors matter in new media*. Institute of Network Cultures.

Van Dijk, Teun A. 2001. "Critical discourse analysis." in *The handbook of discourse analysis*, edited by Deborah Tannen, Heidi Ehernberger Hamilton, and Deborah Schiffrin, pp. 349–371. Malden: Wiley Blackwell.

Wallenstein, Andrew. 2017. "Reed hastings doesn't want 'the get down' cancellation to discourage Netflix." *Variety*. May 31, 2017. http://variety.com

Wayne, Michael L. 2018. "Netflix, Amazon, and branded television content in subscription video On-demand portals." *Media, Culture & Society* 40(5), 725–741.

Weedon, Chris. 1997. *Feminist practice & Poststructuralist Theory*. Chapel Hill: Armadillo Books.

Wolff, Michael. 2017. *Television is the New Television: The Unexpected Triumph of Old Media in the Digital Age*. New York: Penguin Press.

Zuboff, Shoshana. 2019. *The Age of Surveillance Capitalism: The fight for a Human Future at the New Frontier of power*. New York: Public Affairs.

Index

About the Author

Colin Jon Mark Crawford is a PhD student in the Film and Moving Image program at Concordia University, Montréal. His current research examines the new discourses and temporalities of value driving the expansion of platform television as an emergent amalgam of culture, technology, and finance industries.

CPSIA information can be obtained
at www.ICGtesting.com
Printed in the USA
LVHW080750290822
726885LV00012B/338